Lynn Dee & David,

Hope the pages of my
Dream Come True inspire you!

Selena

COURAGE
is ABUNDANT
in the ABSTRACT

COURAGE
is ABUNDANT
in the ABSTRACT

Take your dreams
from **ABSTRACT** to **REALITY**

Selena Einwechter

Published by Deeds Publishing in Athens, GA

www.deedspublishing.com

Printed in The United States of America

Cover design and text layout by Mark Babcock.

Library of Congress Cataloging-in-Publications data is available upon request.

ISBN 978-1-944193-31-7

Books are available in quantity for promotional or premium use. For information, email info@deedspublishing.com.

First Edition, 2016

10 9 8 7 6 5 4 3 2 1

Dedication

Dear Reader,

In the opening chapter of this book, I mention a friend who told me, "Selena, if there is something that has been on your heart for so long that you just can't seem to shake it, well then, it might just be from God."

That friend's name is Tracy Johnston Benden. Our lives were woven together in 1995 as we both built homes and started new life chapters in Atlanta. Our friendship was sparked by the love of walking our four-legged children in our neighborhood. From there we embarked on parallel journeys of fun, faith, and dreams come true.

Tracy was the one person in my life who had the ability to convey messages from God. She knew it and so did I. This didn't happen often, but when it did we were both taken aback. She was a gift from God who helped me transform my vision from simply wanting to be an innkeeper to showing hospitality to strangers. Tracy is one of the most loving and centered people I have ever met, and she had a battalion of friends unlike any other.

Tracy and I were "running buddies" for more than ten years. She was involved with so many of my initiatives — from the creation of Dreambuilders to Creative Gifts to our Buckwiser Investment Group. Through it all, she took me seriously — I would come up with starry-eyed ideas and she would step onboard, help breathe them into existence, and nudge my dream along.

During our time as friends, our journeys paralleled with the ongoing discovery of our individual faith and dreams. In November 2009, we both celebrated our dreams coming true — mine was the Bed & Breakfast on Tiffany Hill and Tracy's was the birth of her daughter.

When Tracy hugged you, you knew you were loved. She had a powerful impact on so many lives, yet no one truly knew how many she had impacted until the stories started pouring in after her death in 2013. Tracy is missed by so many, especially by this dreamer, who might have found her way at some point, but who was encouraged daily by a true friend.

When asked why someone might be interested in reading this book, Tracy replied, "Selena took a leap of faith, trusting in God with her whole heart. People are attracted to leaps of faith, big or small."

The realization of Tiffany Hill took decades and a community of people who continuously encouraged this dreamer each and every step along the path. There are far too many to list here, as it would require another book filled simply with names of people who did their part to inspire me. I know they will all understand my heart as I dedicate this book to Tracy, a friend who is missed so much by so many and will never be forgotten.

"To my dear friend Tracy, another dream realized with the completion of this book! Now I am sharing the story of Tiffany Hill with hopes that I can pass your encouraging ways along by inspiring others to take a step of faith. Thank you for your years of support and encouragement. Each day, each week, each month and year, your words and deeds helped me gain the courage needed to go from the abstract to the real. High five from Tiffany Hill, your friend and running buddy, hugs forever and ever." Selena

Tracy Johnston Benden
Daughter, Friend, Wife, and Mother
1962 to 2013

Introduction

Courage is abundant in the abstract — what does that mean?

It's an intriguing phrase, but what exactly does it mean? For 25 years my courage was abundant in the abstraction of my mind as I talked a good talk — but would I ever actually walk the talk of my dream? My bravery was boundless in the abstract world of my imagination. There, in the sanctuary of my mind, my dream was safe and no one could judge me. Could my actions ever follow? Would I ever push the start button?

For years I talked a good talk with just about anyone and everyone I came in contact with. There was no doubting people knew that I had a dream of opening a bed and breakfast. The question became: Would I? Over the years, my dream haunted me, especially when the dream started aging and friends started to ask if I would ever take that first step.

I could see it, feel it, taste, smell, and touch it — all in my mind, all in the abstract. Sometimes I would "let it out," only to bring it back to the safe zone. Life happened all around my dream, and the pages of time slipped by.

For me, courage was abundant in the abstract!

Faith was abundant in the abstract!

Dreams were abundant in the abstract!

Something in the abstract cannot be felt or experienced by others, as it has no concrete existence. My dreams, courage, and faith were all abstract — easy to talk about, but a bit more difficult to make a reality.

Sure, courage IS abundant when it resides in the abstract! No one can see it, feel it, or touch it. People cannot comment on it one way or the other — it is intangible. No judgment, opinion, or response is required in the abstract. Indeed, the abstract is the comfortable, safe zone for a dreamer. We can dream all we want, day in and day out, with no one but ourselves to evaluate our dream.

The problem with keeping dreams in the abstract is that you might dream away your whole life and never take the first step. Imagine never seeing, feeling, or touching your dream in reality. When my dream stayed out of harm's way, it remained safe — but not fulfilled.

Then, one day I began to think, "But what if?"

That first step of faith helped me become living proof that dreams do come true and courage can also be abundant in reality. I altered my state of my mind to finally let my dreams come out of the safe zone, and soon I started to walk the talk of my dreams. It was only a small step initially, but it was my first step toward building confidence. And that confidence grew with each step, moving in the direction of my dream — creating and crafting it with each movement.

I wish I could snap my fingers and make it really easy for

you to realize your own dream. Or perhaps I could wiggle my nose and then "poof," your dream would unfold in front of your eyes. Unfortunately, it takes a bit more than that.

What I can hopefully do is inspire you with the story of my journey to Tiffany Hill, then lay out some basic principles for creating a business or developing a project so that you can get started on yours. Together we can chart a path that can lead you to the fulfillment of your dream. I not only want to inspire you to begin working toward your goal, I also want to equip you with tools that might lessen the daunting mystery of those first steps.

Along my journey, I read or heard many inspiring stories of people who achieved marvelous things, yet I still didn't take my first step. Sure, my courage was abundant: If other people could achieve their dreams, certainly I could build my bed and breakfast. I would feel on top of the world for a few days until I realized I was exactly where I was before — not knowing what to do first, not knowing the first step to take. I KNEW God wanted me to have the desires of my heart, but how do you go about building a bed and breakfast estate property with very little money in savings? I had to figure it out!

This book you are holding is another step of faith. *Courage is Abundant in the Abstract* shares my journey to the Bed & Breakfast on Tiffany Hill from three perspectives: courage, faith, and dreams. It starts with my successful transformation of my abstract dream into reality. I then outline tangible steps to start you on a path of realizing your dream. And finally, I relate some stories of others who have been inspired by my experience at Tiffany Hill.

Courage is Abundant in the Abstract is in itself a step toward taking a new dream out of the safe zone. You see, I am not a writer! But I felt compelled to share the story of Tiffany Hill to hopefully inspire others to walk toward their dreams and goals. Courage is Abundant in the Abstract is a new step of courage for me that will hopefully inspire courage in you.

How do you go about writing a book? One word at a time. And so it begins.

1.
Courage is Abundant in the Abstract

Life is a blank palette.
It is what you choose to make of it that counts.

No matter how old you are, you might be just like me. On the inside I always felt like a little girl with a big ol' dream. Sparked on a three-month backpack trip across Europe staying at bed and breakfasts, my 25-year dream could not be shaken. A dear friend once told me, "Selena, if there is something that has been on your heart for so long that you just can't seem to shake it, it might just be from God."

As I pondered the thought that this big ol' dream might be from the Man upstairs, I wondered how I could deny what God intended for me to do. What had kept me from moving forward in faith? Fear! Courage lies on the other side of fear. This was a defining moment: realizing that my dream was not simply something I wanted to do, but it was something God wanted me to do. My friend gave me the encouragement to trust God's message to me, take a leap of faith, and turn my abstract dream into my new reality.

Do you have a dream? Is there something you have been thinking about that you cannot seem to shake? Do you have a vision of something? A goal to reach?

Between Facebook, the evening news, sports programs, and our social circles, we often hear about people who have done miraculous things or who have achieved great successes. Often they give the glory to God and you might wonder, "Did God forget about me?" Not at all! God's gifts come in all shapes and sizes. In most of those stories you hear of or read about, those people DID something! The accomplishment was not just given to them on a silver platter.

Open yourself up to God's lead. He wants you to have the desires of your heart, but you must meet Him on the path. It takes an equal alliance: His message and your action. You are His tangible human walking this Earth purposed to make it happen. In partnership, you can take a step of faith toward your dream.

Our ideas come from Him, but it is up to us whether we choose to act on them or not. Fear and doubt often cause us to dismiss our ideas or downsize them to fit our consciousness. God has freely given the idea and we can create something big, something small, or nothing at all. It is our response to His ideas that will define who we are.

Consider this analogy: If you go to the ocean to get water, the water will fill whatever container you choose to use. If you choose a thimble, you will gain a thimbleful. But if you take a large bucket, you will collect a bounty in comparison. It is up to you. We all have free will to choose how we will live our lives. Trust God to lead and guide you toward what is necessary to manifest your dreams.

Your first step of faith does not have to be a total investment of your life savings. Not at all! Much of my initial journey cost nothing but my time: a little research, volunteering in the industry, even launching a savings plan. You'll find that once you start the process, your momentum will mount with each new experience you gain.

Knowledge will help fuel your confidence and propel you to take another step. Using the resources in your library, the business community, or even online will fill you with information and ideas. Soon you will be writing a business plan, developing a financial plan, and creating a project implementation plan. These important elements will cost you nothing but time and before you know it, you will be talking the talk of your future. It's time to recognize the importance of dreams in your life.

Focus is Key!

If something is important to you, you will have to focus on it for it to come to pass. There will always be distractions. There will never be a perfect time. There will be a million things that will jump in your way to steer you in a different direction — from the busyness of daily life to feedback from friends about your journey. It is much easier to lose focus than it is to keep it. This is really natural. Take it all in. Breathe. Make your dream a picture in your mind. The only one who will KNOW if something is right or wrong for you and your life's direction is you. You must stay focused with your eye on the vision you are trying to reach. Soon, your mind will steer you back on point automatically.

The best way to do this is to begin with the end in sight. The Bed & Breakfast on Tiffany Hill is the manifestation of my dream come true. Nestled in the foothills of Western North Carolina, perched on top of a hill, Tiffany Hill welcomes guests from around the world who want to enjoy mountains and waterfalls, the Blue Ridge Parkway, the Brevard Music Festival, the Flat Rock Playhouse, the Biltmore Estate, and the quaint villages in the greater Asheville area.

When guests walk into the Bed & Breakfast on Tiffany Hill, it is fun to watch their faces as we introduce them to my Dream Come True. Typically, the wife will be in awe of the beautiful decor and Southern charm. You know she is sold on her stay the moment she crosses the threshold. In our introduction, we then mention that Tiffany Hill is a purpose-built new construction bed and breakfast designed with guests in mind. At this point we can actually see the wheels of thought moving as the husband starts considering how it all came together, one wall at a time. Or, perhaps they both might be impressed by the fact that the business itself was created from scratch.

Now that I have their attention, here comes the "shock and awe" part: And I built this as a single person! What?

Did I do it alone? Of course not! There is NO WAY that I could have built this million-dollar property on my own — none! It took years of focus, perseverance, determination, and a lot of prayer. It took a community of people who encouraged me every step of the way. It took a little girl laying down her will for something she wanted so badly and for so long to finally release it to God. As I said before, He wants you to have the desires of your heart — but you have to be willing to lay your will at His feet to confirm that this is truly His will for your life. Not the other way around.

We are all purposed for this life. You are NOT a mistake. God created you to be in this world for a reason — or for several reasons along life's journey. Probably the most peace I have felt in all my whole life is when I've delighted in the knowledge that I am doing exactly what God put me on this earth to do — to show hospitality to strangers.

Have you ever dreamed of owning a bed and breakfast? Many have. How nice it would be to entertain guests! You would meet amazing people who have incredible life stories. You will hear about places they have travelled, sights they have seen, and experiences they have had. You will get to know them and become friends with many. You will have fun cooking, making breakfast, and becoming a tour guide as you help others discover fun things to do in your area. While guests are away, you might dream of being in the gardens or maybe baking cookies. All of it, so much fun!

Have you ever imagined opening your own business or building a business from the ground up? I'm not talking about retrofitting an existing building to meet your needs, but creating exactly the structure you've always envisioned instead. You buy the property, work with an architect, and then watch as your vision rises up from the ground — something you made, you created!

Innkeeping is my dream and I am having the time of my life. But not everyone is cut out to be an innkeeper. It might seem like a charmed existence, but you have to be willing to love everyone who comes through the door, adapt to their varied requests, clean up after them, and smile when something you know you will never be able to replace is broken. No, not everyone is made for innkeeping, But everyone is made for something. Finding what God designed you to do on this earth will be the single most important and freeing event of your life. You will have arrived!

Ordinary People Do Extraordinary Things

First, I need to make something abundantly clear. This little girl with a big dream is a very ordinary person, no different than most you who are reading this book. Ordinary comes in all shapes and sizes these days. This ordinary girl is a product of a broken home with lots of challenges along life's path. Those challenges shaped me, molded my character, and helped me to ultimately realize my dream. As I look back in the rear-view mirror of my life, it all makes sense. Each and every challenge, growth spurt, struggle, experience, and so on was perfectly planned to bring me to the point where I am today. We all have our own journey full of experiences. At times I wish that I had seen my journey a bit more clearly as I was going through it. Perhaps then I would have arrived earlier. But each of our paths unfolds at the time appointed. Our task is to be thankful for the points of clarity and for arriving at our dreams when we do!

The difference between that ordinary girl with a big, 25-year dream and the current innkeeper of the Bed & Breakfast on Tiffany Hill is realizing that I have a Big God on my team. How in the world did a virtually penniless woman go from working in corporate America for 31 years to building a successful bed and breakfast in Western North Carolina? When I look back on the media attention the off-the-beaten-path Bed & Breakfast on Tiffany Hill garnered in five short years, I am astounded! It is easy to grab the attention of local media when a business opens or even when you pass your one-year anniversary. Beyond those initial milestones, Tiffany Hill has been featured in:

• *Inns,* August 2009
• *EveryDay with Rachel Ray,* February 2011

- *Southern Lady,* June 2012
- *Southern Living,* August 2012
- *Our State*, August 2012
- *Money*, December 2012
- CNN, December 2012
- *Wall Street Journal*, March 2014
- Named the first bed and breakfast in the *Southern Living* Hotel Collection, June 2014.

There is no way that this little girl could garner that kind of attention by myself! I'm telling you, God's plans for you are far bigger and greater than you could ever imagine. He will orchestrate what needs to happen — and by whom — as long as you are open and willing to do His will.

To punctuate that point, from the day I opened Tiffany Hill, I have always said that my dream was inspired by the pages of Southern Living. What good Southern woman doesn't rip pages out of the magazine for inspiration in decor, food, garden, and travel? My goal was to have Southern Living discover Tiffany Hill and write a full feature story. To that end, a grassroots guerilla marketing effort to get the magazine to take notice was initiated. I asked my guests to write letters to the editor about their experience on the Hill. After a year's worth of letters, the editor's assistant contacted me and said, "Ok, Selena, we know you are there. You can call off your campaign." Guess we got their attention!

So in August of 2011, the Bed & Breakfast on Tiffany Hill received her "big" article, a one-paragraph inclusion in a broader travel story called "Have the Time of Your Life" about a trip from Lake Lure to Highlands, North Carolina. It may not have been the full-length feature I had hoped for, but Tiffany Hill was indeed highlighted with a spotlight on our three-course gourmet breakfast.

This part of the story does not end with this magazine article, though. Fast-forward to our fifth anniversary celebration where Southern Living's representative was present to announce that the Bed & Breakfast on Tiffany Hill would be the first bed and breakfast included in their new Southern Living Hotel Collection. Think about that for a moment! There are hundreds — if not thousands — of bed and breakfasts in the South. How in the world did this happen? That answer is easy — God! From the beginning of the inspirational pages being torn from the monthly publications, He knew that in 2013, this Hotel Collection would be formed and He was going to orchestrate Tiffany Hill's inclusion. Bigger and grander than I could have ever dreamed!

The Beginning of a Dream

Before there was breakfast, there was a dream. The seeds of my dream were planted more than 25 years ago. One never knows what event in your past might have been the spark to ignite your dream or God's plan for your life.

As we journey through the years, God orchestrates our experiences to equip us for future work. For example, who knew that my government stint as a white-collar crime investigator in land fraud would provide me the confidence I needed to review restrictive covenants when I purchased the property now called Tiffany Hill? Or how the time I spent staging special events for the Florida Lottery would sharpen my hospitality and event skills? Not to mention that all my time in various management positions with different departments reporting to me would help hone my ability to multi-task and wear all of the hats of an innkeeper.

Most importantly, the five lottery start-up projects I participated in perfected my skills as a project manager. Those projects most certainly prepared me for my business startup, in which I not only needed to make sure all the elements of the B&B construction were completed, the rooms decorated, guest amenities put in place, food stocked for breakfast—but I also needed a website up and running, complete with a reservation booking engine, marketing materials had to be printed, and everything had to be operational by opening day.

Looking back, I am amazed at the journey I took and how He perfectly designed my life so that I was completely equipped to do the task at hand. In other words, God supplies you when He calls you. He doesn't always call the equipped; He equips the called.

This Big Ol' Dream of mine incubated for decades. The first introduction I had to the bed and breakfast experience was backpacking in Europe as a starving college graduate who was determined to step her feet on the land where she was born, Wiesbaden, Germany. Camping was not my thing, nor did I have a good experience with visiting youth hostels. That's when the discovery of B&Bs happened. A bed and breakfast provided a place where you could have a wonderful night's rest and a solid meal to start your new day. Little did I know that at that point God was busy planting the seeds of my future!

Life unfolded. My corporate career took off and we do what we do when we find a comfortable rhythm of life — we work day in and out to support ourselves, and then we jam in a little fun on the weekends or whenever we are not working. For me, that meant planning trips to B&Bs in the New England area — until I discovered they were in my backyard in the South as well.

From there, I started going to industry conferences. I was labeled an "aspiring innkeeper," "B&B Wannabe," and also targeted as someone who might buy somebody's existing B&B business. The dream percolated as I learned to wear this new label. I shared it with friends — and with just about anyone who would listen. I became obsessed with this dream of mine. With each experience, each conference, and each B&B visit, I grew more confident and I knew I could do it. I devised plans on top of plans to get to where I needed to go, one right after another. But alas, we are so human! And sometimes we are so wrong.

Do Something — Anything to Move Closer!

For years, my courage remained abundant in the abstract as I concocted all sorts of projects and initiatives to gain knowledge in areas I was unfamiliar with or to simply encourage myself and grow my confidence. I was always talking about having a B&B, but never seemed to do anything about it.

In 1999, I watched a documentary about a young man who wanted to make a film. He asked 10 people for $1,000, and he ended up winning an award at a film festival. What a great idea! So that same year, I launched the Dreambuilders Fund. I sent letters to all my friends and family seeking encouragement and asking for $100 in return for a gift certificate for a free night at my future B&B (location yet to be determined).

As the donations rolled in, I would send a beautiful reservation certificate accompanied by a heartfelt letter of gratitude. I will never forget the very first Dreambuilder, a dear friend and my professional mentor. I was in her office one morning when I decided to bounce my blossoming idea off her. In an instant she whipped her chair around, grabbed her wallet, and wrote a check for $100. The Dreambuilder Fund was launched.

First Dreambuilder Letter

September 1999
Dear friends and family,

For as long as I can remember, I have had this dream... come, let me share it with you. Imagine...in my dream, a country lane lined with white fencing. As you continue, a house begins to reveal itself. You are immediately taken with the inviting wrap around porch of this country Victorian farmhouse. You spot several rocking chairs, which seem to be calling your name, and make a mental appointment to sit a while. As you stand on the porch, you turn to view the pastoral setting: peaceful and relaxing. You have arrived to my dream — to my country inn... stay awhile!

I have been researching the country inn/bed and breakfast industry for many years; attending seminars and conferences, as well as visiting inns whenever I can. Five years ago, I set a goal to have an inn at the end of five years. But wishing and wanting didn't make my dream come true. Recently, I was inspired by a story of a struggling filmmaker who made his dream a reality through individual supporters. He asked people for small amounts which, when combined, gave him the funding he needed to succeed. What a great idea! Asking the multitudes for support might be the key to my dream coming true!

But "never ask for something for nothing"! For every $100

of support, you will receive a reservation certificate good for a luxurious night at the inn. Supporters of $500 can stay the week! The more people, the better! Just think how impressive it will be when I take my "Supporter List" to the bank seeking financing and show them how many guests are ready to come to the inn.

Over the next five years, I will be working diligently to turn this dream into a reality and need specific individuals who encourage dream builders. As a supporter, you will receive an annual newsletter with updates on the progress of our venture together. In the meantime, all contributions received will be held in the Dream Fund, which has been established at Bank One.

Success is a journey of many steps and the writing of this letter is an important step in building this dream.

Looking forward to seeing you at the inn!

By the way, how do you like your eggs?

Selena

This initiative became such a great source of encouragement over the coming years. Imagine the feeling: Checks would arrive in the mailbox from time to time with notes of support. People believed in my dream and in me! They believed in and encouraged me even when, at times, I could not believe in myself nor could I see which way to go. My Dreambuilders gave donations for seven years, until December 2005, when I had

amassed $10,000 in reservation deposits and was feeling un-
sure of where the road was leading.

What an incredible seven-year journey of encouragement this was for this little girl with a big dream. During this
time, I discovered that people enjoy encouraging dreamers. I
also discovered that people actually carried $100 bills in their
pocket — an amazing realization for someone who lived with
a paycheck-to-paycheck mentality. When I founded Tiffany
Hill, Inc., I purposely used the $10,000 in Dreambuilder do-
nations to create the corporation and develop the initial website. The remainder was used as a base of startup capital. Truly,
the Dreambuilders and their collective faith in me became the
foundation that this dream was built on.

Over the years I attended all sorts of B&B conferences and
workshops designed for aspiring innkeepers. At one of those
B&B Wannabe seminars, the main takeaway was that a million dollars was just another zero, i.e., $100,000+0. That was
an interesting perspective but a huge jump from saving pennies and dollars in order to add that one zero! I also learned
there were three ways to enter the business: buy an existing
B&B with an established reputation (good or bad), purchase
a building and convert it to a B&B, or build one from the
ground up.

That was an easy decision for me as I did not want someone
else's reputation nor would I want to convert an old structure.
No, building from the ground up and creating my own brand

with my own reputation was clearly the direction I would take. No one could talk me out of it either. My mind was set.

So, in an effort to gain experience, in the mid 1990s I decided to build a home in Atlanta. My first entry into new construction offered several floor plans, three choices of this or that, with very few custom change options. This was a far cry from creating a custom floor plan for a B&B like Tiffany Hill, but constructing my little house was still a confidence-builder nonetheless. Another step in the journey.

From a financial perspective, I knew that building a bed and breakfast from the ground up was going to take a lot more money than I had saved over the years. So in 1998, I became determined to learn about the stock market and how to grow my nest egg.

Taking a page from the renowned Beardstown Ladies Investment Club, I invited four friends to invite three of their friends to join our lady's investment club, and before you knew it, the BuckWisers Investment Club was launched. This was a very low-risk, $25-a-month, education-based investment social club with the goal of learning how to grow our money. We kept the club for several years and gleaned so much together! Most importantly, we learned that if you wanted to have your money grow, you had to have disposable money—funds that you did not need for daily living and were willing to risk if you lost them.

There are two ways to have disposable money, either to make more or to spend less. I was determined to do both! With the help of a financial consultant, I figured out what I would need to put away over the course of the next seven or more years in order to save $350,000 in disposable income and not impact my retirement. We went back and forth for weeks, and at times I know she thought I had lost my mind! But when we were done, I knew exactly what I needed to do each year, each month, and each week to save for my dream. Which meant I needed to make more, spend less, and sock what I could away.

I started with the money I received from tax returns, increased my savings every time I received a raise, and created a sideline business of making stained-glass gifts and selling them at shows. I even created a holiday gift show sale called Creative Gifts and Fabulous Finds, hosted in my own home each holiday season. Customers would line up for the opening hour so that they would be the first to see what unique gifts my friends and I had created. Such fun! This show had an eight-year run and certainly helped grow the savings plan.

During that time, I also diligently (and creatively!) worked on spending less so that I could save more. My motto was "Frugal is Fun." I was focused and determined to reach my goal. One of the biggest saving initiatives came from digging myself out of debt and living on an all-cash budget. It works! I promise you. There's a tangible difference between swiping a credit card and handing over your hard-earned cash.

The more I saved, the more my money grew. I set up automatic investments in stock market mutual funds with a balance between value stocks and growth stocks. In addition, I laddered CDs in preparation for my first year of business. This meant I purchased a $2,000 monthly CD that would come to term as I left corporate America so that I would have money coming in each month when my income stream eventually stopped.

In the end, my nest egg was making enough that I even questioned why I would cash it all in to build the dream. Was I crazy? After all, I could live on what I had saved at that point for the rest of my life — or so I thought.

A little bit of financial security can be a huge deterrent for pursuing your dream and taking that step of faith. But remain focused! All the money in the world cannot replace the feeling of turning your dream into reality.

Right before I received the corporate boot, I was saving 50 percent of what I made. Yes, 50 percent! One does not wake up one day and go from zero to 50. Slowly but surely, I grew my saving plan from three percent to 50 percent over a period of seven years. My money was finally where my mouth was. That savings plan ultimately provided the financial pathway to fulfill my dream. Keep in mind, I started saving at least seven years before I received my walking papers — not the day I lost my job. My best advice is to start today — this very minute — for what you envision for your future.

Volunteer in the Industry

Over that period of saving, I was also hard at work doing what cost little in the form of money, but was invaluable as a confidence-builder. I had a floor plan, business plan, logo, and marketing plan; the dream was taking shape. For a while there, I even felt like it was on automatic pilot. You cannot make time fly (although it often seems to do so on its own). I had to wait patiently for the savings plan to grow.

But there was one last thing I could do to prepare — I could volunteer! If I volunteered at a B&B, I knew I would gain insight and experience that would help me KNOW if this dream life was for me. So during one of my B&B excursions, I made an offer that hopefully the then-owner of the Secret Garden Bed & Breakfast in Weaverville, North Carolina could not refuse.

If she would show me how to operate her inn, I would be happy to take it over for free whenever she wanted to go on vacation. Imagine her reaction after meeting me all of maybe two hours prior! She was slowly, but surely, backing up politely to escape this conversation! She did not know me or my character. Could I be trusted with her dream? The Secret Garden was a sweet three-bedroom operation that I felt comfortable cutting my teeth on. Hoping that she might feel a connection and take a chance on me, I made my final pitch at breakfast the next morning. To my delight, she responded that she, too, felt a connection! From that moment on, we launched a wonderful friendship. I would commute on the weekends from Atlanta whenever I could to help her. My first B&B mentor took me under her wing and showed me how to run her dream. What a wonderful journey of friendship and trust.

When the time came for me to make good on my offer and take over her bed and breakfast, I was a nervous wreck! I got through that weekend figuring out what I did not know and winging the rest. My lifelong motto of "fake it till you make it" helped me through, but just barely. With her coaching over the next few years, my confidence grew.

She sold her B&B a few years into our friendship and I was devastated. But an ending typically creates a new beginning. Our next venture was formed: inn-sitting for other B&Bs in the Asheville area. What a wonderful way to see other operations this was. I learned so much and saw such a variety of styles of doing business in the B&B industry. This helped me pick and choose different elements that I would incorporate into my own operation one day. It also helped build my confidence to see a variety of people who were not necessarily brighter or wealthier than I running their own bed and breakfasts. I will never forget Cassandra Clark's mentorship, which showed me that a single woman could in fact run her own B&B operation with grace and style. I am forever in her debt.

Something Missing...

I was busy living life, working at my job, and pining for my Dream Come True. I was making all my plans move forward, but something was totally missing: God!

From the night I spent in my first B&B in Europe through my inn-sitting experiences at the Secret Garden, God was not a part of my story. At least I didn't realize that He was. I was merrily going along my path doing whatever I could think of to transition my dream from the abstract to the real.

Then one day, on my way to work, I received a call from one of the staff about the planes crashing into the World Trade Center. It was September 11, 2001. I hurried into the office to do what we all did that fateful day, watch the devastation of people's lives unfold on TV. The realization of our own in-security and the raw emotions to which those terrible events gave rise sent many of us to the only place we hoped to find an-swers — church. I knew there had to be more to life than all the things we fill our time with, including the making of a dream.

As I attended church Sunday after Sunday, searching for comfort and answers, a passage in Psalms was revealed to me:

"Unless the Lord builds the house, those who build it labor in vain." Psalm 127:1

How in the world do you let God build your house? How could He build my B&B? Yet I knew in that moment that if I did it with my own might, as I had done with so many other things in my life, it would fail. If God built it, it would succeed. It was there in black and white. I knew it was true. I had no option but to let God build this dream of mine.

His Will vs. Your Will

So I went about trying to figure out how to release and lay down this dream of mine . . . totally and completely, so that God had room to move in. Exactly how do you go about doing that? How do you let go of something that you have been developing in your mind for decades? Something that you have organized your whole life around? The very thing that defines who you are? Laying that down is much easier said than done!

I sought the advice of my ministers, knowing surely they had counseled someone on this before and would know exactly how to direct me. Their answer to me was to "pray about it." Oh that's good, I thought . . . no, no, there had to be a more definitive answer for this. So off I went to the bookstore looking for answers on how to lay down your will. Nothing gave me what I was seeking. But I KNEW that laying down my will was exactly what I had to do. I had no choice. I had to figure it out. So pray I did.

Each day I prayed the same prayer, "Take my will from me; Your will be done." I prayed in the morning. I prayed at night. I would journal about it. Whenever my dream floated into my head, I tried to release it and give it up to the Lord. Let me paint a picture here: I am not someone who lands on her knees every night to pray before I go to sleep (although I should). My prayer life with God is more of a conversation with a friend. But over the coming months, I continued to pray the same prayer. There was a time or two that I thought I had laid down my will. I could actually feel my grip release and feel myself letting go of my dream, opening up to what God would do with me. Then suddenly I would get scared and mentally say, "NOPE, no way!" I'd grab my dream back and hold it tight. How could I release what I had dreamed of for so long and so hard? No, no, no! Back to praying again every day.

Then one morning it happened: The first tangible communication I received from God. I was driving to work along the same route I followed five days a week. How can I describe what happened? The best I can say is that there was an "essence" in the passenger seat. That "essence" conveyed to me that I was going in the right direction. That was it! That's all I got! After a year of praying the same prayer daily, there was my answer. As ambiguous as it might appear, I received a knowledge in the depth of my soul that I was going in the right direction. I knew that I was on the right path, so I continued. It was the affirmation I needed. It surpassed all understanding. I had at that moment laid down my will and His will for my life stepped in. I would trust in Him to lead and I would follow.

Willing Servant — Don't Make it Too Complicated

So I got busy. The focus of my journey shifted from a fun Polly-anna dream of running a B&B to an actual "knowing" that this was God's will for my life. If it was His will, then I better get busy knowing Him better. The mental shift took me from what I wanted to do to wanting what He wanted me to do. I became diligent in my studies of the Word; I took five years of Disciple training, became a layperson Stephen Minister, and went on the Walk to Emmaus.

Then, after seven years of preparation and study, I found myself at the altar crying. People from all walks of life — and all faiths — would be dining at my future B&B table, and I felt like I needed to be able to answer any question that any guest might ask about the Bible. What an overwhelming thought! Despite seven years of study, I wasn't able to recite scripture, nor was I an authority on the Word. What else did I need to do to prepare for this dream, which was now evolving into a ministry? The answer was simple, really: I needed a change in my perspective.

As I sat there crying my eyes out, someone came over to comfort me. I poured out my heart's dilemma to them. The answer was easy; all I really needed to do was be a willing servant. Be an instrument of God. He will equip you in all you do if you allow Him to work through you. Seek discernment in all situations, and then simply be a willing servant.

At that moment, the heavy burden of what I had put on

myself — to have all the answers — was totally and completely lifted. My intensive seven years of biblical study was not for nothing, however. It was clearly a time of preparation for me to grow spiritually and prepare my heart for what He had in store. I was ready to apply my faith to the seeds of the dream planted decades prior. At this juncture, my dream and His Will for my life were married. Oh heavenly day!

Board Meeting with God

At this point things started to fast-track. In the spring of 2007, the timetable for opening Tiffany Hill was put in place. I knew I needed to open by early summer 2009. I put the finishing touches on the business plan. Living with a "paycheck to paycheck" mentality, I already had a savings plan that had been stepped up every time a raise came my way or new money appeared. I had developed a marketing plan and strategy. The company logo was complete. The floor plan was designed. My magazine tear sheets were catalogued into a building portfolio of ideas. I even had a brochure created that depicted each suite so that I could better communicate my abstract vision to others.

Yet there was still an item missing that I knew I needed — a Project Implementation Plan. It had been on my "to do" list for years. Funny, I did these types of plans in my daily job all the time. Why could I not seem to do this for my dream?

Tired of bearing the weight of this burden, I came to a point where it was going to happen that very weekend or I was going to drop this dream of mine. I wanted to shake what had been driving me crazy for years. What was I afraid of? If I put the plans into a project timeline, would I fear failure if the timeline was not met? Or was it seeing it for myself in concrete terms that was keeping me from that project plan? At this point, with a growing nest egg, I even started thinking, "Maybe I didn't need to do this B&B dream. I could easily live happily ever after on what I have saved."

So on a Saturday morning, I fired up the computer in my home office, clicked the green icon for Microsoft Project, and stared at the screen waiting for the Project Implementation Plan to appear. In that very instant, before I could type a word, a dear friend called and could tell I was wound tight as a rubber band. "What is up with you?" she asked. Out poured my thoughts in a "pissy" way. I told her that I was one unfinished document away from throwing away my dreams.

My dear friend patiently replied, "You need to shut down that computer and go have a board meeting with God!" Board meeting with God? Exactly how do you do something like that? That was one of the silliest things I ever heard. "Take your Bible to your dining room table," she said, "and open it."

Amazingly, this stubborn girl who never likes to be told what to do did exactly that. For the next six to eight hours, I went through one of my Bibles and marked everything that seemed to speak to me. Afterwards, I pulled out my journal and started to write. Typically, I would journal a page at a time, but not this day. Instead I wrote for pages and pages on end but did not complete the last page in full as I typically do. I got midway through that page and I was done. I had poured my heart out in that journal. And then it happened. It was as if God picked up the pen and wrote to me:

My stubborn child, it is not you who gave me your will, but I who have given you My will for your life. All that I ask is that you stop along the journey — pray and listen.

Instantly, I dropped that pen and said, as any good military daughter would say to her father, "Sir, yes Sir!" It almost scared me to death!

The next morning I skipped church and fired up the computer. In three short hours (compared to the years of procrastination) the multi-tiered, interdependent Project Implementation Plan was complete! I knew exactly what had to be done and when each task needed to be completed so that God and I could accomplish this dream by a specific date. What had haunted me for years was finally complete. Once again I was shown that if I pushed through with my own will and determination, I would not succeed. That board meeting with God clearly showed me that only when you fully rely on God in all things will such roadblocks be overcome.

Even though I had embarked on a spiritual path which revealed that my dream was His will for my life, I still went about "my" dream, busy doing things, and from time to time I left Him out. I had all those plans and materials, but I was busy in parallel with God, not truly with God. A huge difference! I was not involving Him in all I did. Big mistake! From that point forward, He was involved in it all — my co-designer, my co-builder, my co-pilot. I looked for Him at every turn. I knew we were in this journey together. He was my ultimate partner.

From Abstract to Reality

The path to the realization of your dream will almost never be straight. It seems like the closer you move toward the reality, the more jagged the journey can become. Let me dig deeper for just a moment and go back to a time when I almost threw in the towel.

Later that same year, in 2007, when I was right at the brink of taking that final leap of faith to pursue my dream, the worst thing imaginable for a single person with one source of income happened. After 31 years working for governments and corporations, I was given what I call the "corporate boot" — my very own pink slip. Oh no! I had already hired a real estate company in Western North Carolina to look for property and I had begun talking to builders. I was on my way to Tiffany Hill — my dream was coming true!

But an Italian company purchased my U.S.-based company, took a good look at the organizational charts, and trimmed mid-management positions. It was a defining fork in the road for me as I battled with which direction to turn. Do I look for another position in my industry, a choice that would most certainly delay my dream? Or do I dare take that first big step of faith toward my dream? I have to admit I was devastated for the first three days. I cried a river. How was a single, 53-year-old woman going to build a million-dollar dream while unemployed? The plan had always been to build while I was still working, then transition to the dream. No one would loan me a million dollars without a job!

So here I was at my defining moment. I had to choose. I could certainly talk the talk in the security of my safe little world of earning a paycheck, paying my bills, and living my life. But now I was at the point of stepping into the unknown reality of my dream without a job. All the plans I'd made were completed in a comfort zone of employment. No true risk involved. Again, courage is abundant in the abstract. But faith is also so abundant in the abstract!

Could I truly put my faith into action and walk the talk of my dream? Would I be able to put my faith in action, trust the Creator, and walk the walk with everything on the line?

If the truth were known, in the recesses of my mind I believe I was waiting on my Prince Charming to come make it all happen. I had the plans, but I needed financing and I needed a partner. How could I bring this to pass on my own?

At this pivotal point in my journey, a dear friend gave me the book *As a Man Thinketh* by James Allen. This classic essay teaches the profound power of our own thoughts.

There may have been tangible and intangible forces that

propelled my dream toward my new reality, but reading this book was the single most pivotal moment in the battlefield of my mind. At my lowest point — unemployed, 53, single, with a feeling of my million-dollar dream going up in smoke — I read the following passage:

All that a man achieves and all that he fails to achieve is the direct result of his own thoughts. In a justly ordered universe, where loss of equipoise would mean total destruction, individual responsibility must be absolute. A man's weakness and strength, purity and impurity are his own, and not another man's, they are brought about by himself and not by another and they can only be altered by himself, never by another. His condition is also his own, and not another man's. His suffering and his happiness are evolved from within. As he thinks, so he is, as he continues to think, so he remains.

"For as he thinks within himself, so he is."
—Proverbs 23:7

Until thought is linked with purpose there is no accomplishment. Aimlessness is a vice. Conceive a legitimate purpose and set out to accomplish it. You will overcome weakness and gain strength of character. Mentally mark out a straight pathway —thoughts of fear and doubt never accomplish anything and never can.

She who conquers fear and doubt has conquered failure. Thought allied with purpose becomes creative force. All that a woman achieves and all that she fails to achieve is a direct result of her own thoughts. The dreamers are the saviors of the world. My vision is the promise of what one day I will be. My ideal is the prophecy of what I will unveil. Dreams are seedlings of realities.

How powerful James Allen's words are, and written in 1903! For generations, we all experience the same human challenges of having courage in the abstract. As I read this passage, it felt like an invisible barrier in the battlefield of my mind had been pierced, and suddenly I was on the other side of my "courage is abundant in the abstract" dilemma. I danced with joy! If it was going to happen, it was up to me to take the next tangible step toward my new reality. As far as Prince Charming — well, he'd been there all along. My Prince Charming was God! We would make this happen together — I was not alone.

"Commit your ways to the Lord, trust in Him and He will bring it to pass." Psalm 37:5

The battlefield of my mind was settling, but I'd lost my focused direction in those days of devastation after my job loss. What should be my next step? On the third day after my pink slip, I found myself in one of my pastors' offices wringing my hands, not knowing what to do. She asked me about the length of my severance package, then said, "Why don't you take half that time and pursue your dream as hard as you can, then at the midway point evaluate where you are?" WOW! Great advice! Her words took the immediate pressure of looking for another job off of me. I had three and a half months, half my severance period, to pursue my dream as hard as I could and find the location for Tiffany Hill.

Thankfully my Project Implementation Plan had been completed before I lost my job. I simply pulled that out and knew what tangible steps to take next. The real estate search that had already begun went into full gear, and three and a half months later — to the very day — I stepped foot on the property that would become Tiffany Hill.

Looking back, at first all I could see was the devastation of losing my job and my dream going up in smoke. But the ending of my corporate career created a whole new stepping-off point in faith. Indeed, new beginnings come from some other beginning's end. Perspective is all in how you look at things. Isn't God awesome? He gave me the safety net of seven months of severance to help me feel financially secure. Plus, what a blessing it was to have the unexpected time to throw myself completely into my dream without the distraction of a day job.

With a plan in place, God had prepared me to walk confidently in the direction of my dreams. One step at a time.

There Will Be Challenges

The first faithful step into the unknown is monumental, but don't think the whole process of achieving my dream was a bowl of cherries. There were times I felt like giving up. It is not easy to walk in faith just because you have made the decision to step out. Take plumbing, for example! At one point in the building process I was given a 30-page document listing all the plumbing elements I needed to approve, including part numbers and other bits and pieces. What? Show me a picture and I might know what on earth you are wanting me to understand and approve. But I figured it out!

Another challenge came during the construction process, when it rained for 40 days and 40 nights. Mud was everywhere — and it was being tracked through this beautiful structure being built. What a mess! God, did I misread your call? Was I supposed to build the second ark instead of a bed and breakfast? Surely we were going to be washed away!

Then there was the time when installers were scheduled to lay the carpet that had been carefully selected six months prior to the B&B opening date. A week prior to my first guest arriving, the company called to let me know that someone failed to check the color when it arrived in their warehouse months prior. Would I accept purple carpet? You must be kidding — purple!

To top everything off, just days before opening Tiffany Hill, our hardwood floors buckled. We could not open closet doors or even the front door for that matter. I have to admit that was not my finest moment. After a collection of people spent hours blaming each other for material defects, the installation, and a laundry list of other excuses, I lost it. Never underestimate the passion of a 5'2" blue-eyed woman! I didn't care if I ripped up the floors with a hammer and put a BIG sign indicating the name of the company responsible. Everyone would see their wonderful workmanship during the upcoming five open houses planned for the following week.

Guess they heard my position clearly as they got busy with huge dehumidifiers, 100-pound weights, and lots of installers making sure that the hardwoods were fitted properly and that the beautiful tan sculpted carpet was installed perfectly by our grand opening.

Indeed, the path isn't always straight. In fact, it's usually not! But take heart. With God on your team, even great challenges — and purple carpet — can be conquered.

God at Work

So, I was doing all I could to make the dream — now God's will for my life — a reality. But what was God doing during this time? Well, He was taking care of the BIG stuff! Let me give you a couple of examples.

When I found the piece of property I now call Tiffany Hill, there was an electrical easement that crossed right through the middle of the six acres. This provided electricity to a whole neighborhood of homes on the other side of the property. The positioning of the lines was right smack dab in the middle of the property. There was no way to position the B&B anywhere that would accommodate those above-ground poles and lines, nor would I want to. Guess what? The power company came out and rerouted the entire span of electrical lines back down to the road, up the other side, and then ultimately buried the lines coming up to the bed and breakfast so that no unsightly overhead lines detracted from the property's beauty. This was all to the tune of maybe $30,000 worth of work, and I didn't have to spend a penny, thanks to God!

Here's another example of His handiwork: Remember the Great Recession that began in 2008? Yes, I lost my job right at the cusp of that economic downturn, on Halloween Day 2007, to be specific. I went about looking for property, found what would become Tiffany Hill in February of 2008, and put the finishing touches on the business plan so that the specific property was included in the proposal, and submitted it to the four lending institutions I had previously identified. These banks included one that had initially approved my plan in the summer of 2007 for 1.2 million dollars. This particular bank was a national bank and one that I had used for the majority of my investment capital. The second bank was a large regional bank that I used for my daily banking and some investments. Of the two other banks, one was regional and the smallest of the four was a local bank. These last two came as recommendations from my real estate agent, based on her knowledge of the local Western North Carolina lending community.

After applying, I waited. And waited. And waited for word from these banks. It felt like watching paint dry. The days of the calendar turned slowly. I turned my attention to other things to pass the time; after all, you cannot push your way into a million-dollar loan. Days turned into weeks and weeks turned into months until finally on a Monday, I received my first call. It was the bank that had vetted the business plan and preliminarily approved me for 1.2 million dollars. Except this time, they were saying no, they would not do the loan.

Another call came in the same day from the large regional bank that I had been banking with for years saying no, they could not do the loan. And then the third call on that fateful day came from the smaller regional bank. As it turns out, they were not extending hospitality loans at this time. Hospitality loans? Ah, a bed and breakfast was defined as a hospitality loan, viewed as a high-risk investment. Had the world turned upside down? No, no, and no. Little did I know at that point that the banks were struggling just before the Great Recession of 2008 hit.

Walking is good therapy at times like these. There's something especially cathartic about putting one foot in front of the other. I took a walk with my dog one morning and it occurred to me that I had done my best. I had pursued my dream as hard as I could. I had been diligent in finding the property, saving my pennies, and putting together a business plan that gained compliments from all of the lending institutions. Finally, I had clarity. If the last bank said "no," I would be released from the dream. I had done my best and that is all God wants from each of us. What a relief — my decision was made.

A couple days passed and finally the fourth call came. It

was the smallest bank — the local bank — ringing to say "yes!" Before I knew it, we were on our way! Purchasing property, finalizing building plans, and timelines — my implementation plan was taking shape and everything was falling into place. I had saved for years and now the direction would shift abruptly from saving to spending.

Over half of my liquid investments needed to be cashed out in order for me to purchase the land outright. The bank wanted me to have "skin in the game," so I needed a cashier's check for $200,000! That was a whole lot of pennies from my perspective. In order to have the cashier's check in time for the June closing I would need to pull money out of the stock market, where I had been faithful in my dollar-cost average investments for years. So in mid-May, just weeks before the stock market plummet of 2008, I pulled the trigger. And thank goodness I did! In hindsight I was very fortunate — God's hand was in this, too. I was truly two weeks away from not having this dream of mine become a reality. Had I waited just two more weeks, my savings nest egg would have been less than half of what was needed to buy the property and build. Talk about God's timing being everything!

The Great Recession did not really affect me. It couldn't! I was on a path with blinders on. Not to mention that I was unemployed and cashing in my life savings for a dream. I can remember a sleepless night before I went to closing with my check in hand. The financial "what if this" and "what if that" kept me up all night! Was I crazy for buying property to build a bed and breakfast? Many thought so! You hear it all the time: being an innkeeper is a 24-hour job, 365 days a year. Why do you want to tie yourself to that? It's exhausting work, etc.

Those thoughts wove their way into my financial stress, and the next morning I was once again second-guessing my decision. I took my dog, Madison, for a walk to try to calm my fears. That is when the third message from God poured over me. God told me that I would have enough. Like the manna in the wilderness, I need not worry. Like the birds in the sky, I need not wonder about what I would eat or where I would find shelter. It was in His hands — and as it turned out, He was right. I had everything I needed. My friends were so generous in their support as the B&B was being built! They delivered meals, brought food for our feral cat Tuxedo, and even supplied seed for the birds. We all had enough.

Once again, His message to me provided a peace that surpassed all understanding. Some people might have thought I was crazy for moving forward. But forward I went to the point of no return, which resulted in the opening of my dream come true, the Bed & Breakfast on Tiffany Hill, on June 5, 2009.

Looking back, I received three messages from God along the journey to Tiffany Hill:

1. The presence in the car that confirmed I was going in the right direction.

2. The time God wrote to me in my journal about His will for my life.
3. The voice of clarity on my walk, assuring me that like the manna in the wilderness, I would have enough.

God's messages were not necessarily direct answers to the questions I had at hand — and I find they rarely are. They didn't even seem to relate exactly to what I was asking or pondering. But, in His great provision, they were all three exactly what I needed: They provided confidence to take the next step on the path, to keep going on the journey with courage and confidence knowing I was doing His will.

You Will Be Tested

Surrendering to God's plan is not just a one-time choice. Rather, it's a life-long process. As much as I thought, "build it and they will come," that did not necessarily happen. My dream had come true. I weathered my corporate layoff, obtained financing, found a builder, purchased furniture for five suites, common areas, and outdoor furnishings. And did another 1,000 things in order to open the doors of Tiffany Hill on schedule June 2009.

Guest reservations were very sparse in 2009 with a recession looming. Everyone was tightening their belts. There were times I would have one couple for just a one-night stay in a two-week span. I kept pouring my own money into Tiffany Hill to keep it afloat. Those early days were scary! How would I keep this business afloat?

To complicate matters, my little bank that walked beside me was having its own problems. The FDIC had come in and many of the people I worked with on the loan had left. My loan process had not been finalized and no one would talk to me. The remaining bank staff reminded me of ostriches with their heads in the sand for fear of misstepping and losing their employment.

Soon my pennies were nearly gone and I did not know what to do or where to turn. I shared this predicament with my best friend. As I reviewed the situation it became clear to me only six months into running my dream that I would need to sell Tiffany Hill. Once again the tears flowed. How could I sell something I had labored over and dreamed about for decades? I loved what I was doing, but the business was not there to support it. I shared the situation with another trusted friend with the same result of tears flowing. The third time I opened up with someone about it, I did not cry. The fact of the matter was that this friend was in a situation where she was struggling with a similar conflict. She needed to release her teenage son to whom she had given birth, had loved, and had worked to shape. It was time to let go so he could lead his own life. What a struggle of passage for parents who have poured their hearts into their children! Releasing anyone or anything that you love is incredibly difficult. This was the case for me and the dream I had birthed on Tiffany Hill and loved with all my heart.

As I shared my dilemma with my friend and ministered to her, I realized that I had grabbed my will back in those six months of operating Tiffany Hill! I was having the time of my life with what God and I had created. Yes, I still recognized God in it, but there was a subtle difference. I was in love with my dream existence, not wanting to lay it down . . . not laying down my will for His. I was holding my dream tight. The light bulb switched on! One can never love something or someone so much that you are not willing to lay it at His feet. That very moment, I released my tightly held grip on Tiffany Hill. The very next week, someone from the bank contacted me. Financial relief was immediate. My lesson was learned.

Within a couple of months, the bank closed my loan and Tiffany Hill was on sound financial footing, at least for a bit. Somehow, some way, we still needed to get Tiffany Hill on the map. Reservations needed to come in. So I prayed. I prayed for one thing every day, consistently — a reservation. Each time we receive a reservation, it was and still is our "blessing" for the day. For seven years running, I have prayed the same prayer. And I watch as God brings those blessings in the form of guests through the front door.

There was a couple who came from Chattanooga for four nights early in November 2009. They were the "king and queen" of Tiffany Hill for the next few days as there were no other guests. After four days, you start to make connections with the guests you serve. Since their first visit in 2009, that very couple has brought a parade of friends who have now experienced what we offer on Tiffany Hill, a place of rest and restoration. In fact, after the first five years, they were responsible for 200+ room nights at the B&B. To me, God used them to help keep the doors of Tiffany Hill open. There is no doubt that God sent them and opened their hearts to support my dream come true. Never underestimate the power of God manifesting itself through the people He brings to your door. Those two individuals helped keep Tiffany Hill afloat during its lean first years.

His Purpose for Your Life

We are all human beings. Never, ever forget that His will for your life is the single most important end point of this journey on earth. We are on this planet for just a blink of time compared to eternity! And you are here for a purpose. When you find that purpose and are working in concert with God, never lose sight that it is His plan for you! We have a natural tendency to get wrapped up in what we do, thinking that we are the motor propelling it forward. Big mistake! Everything we have comes from Him. Here on Tiffany Hill, I strive daily to recognize God in all I do with guests, with staff, and with friends. This is His plan and I am simply a willing servant.

Please do not put God's "call" on your life into a box. So

many people think that a call on someone's life is directly related to a church ministry or traditional mission work. It is clear to
me that God's people are called to be in all walks of life. When I
was in the lottery industry for so many years, I felt shunned by
my church. It took me ages to overcome that perceived stigma. I
actually walked away from my church family because of the veil
of shame I wore working in the lottery industry. Then it dawned
on me — Christians are needed in all walks of life. Matthew was
a tax collector and not liked by many! But yet he became one of
Jesus' most trusted disciples. What has God put on your heart?

At Tiffany Hill, we show "hospitality to strangers." It does
not matter to us what your religion is, what you do for a living,
the stories of your past, or even your present situation. Our
mission is to give you a place of rest and restoration. We are
called to show true, authentic, Christian, Southern hospitality
to our guests. We are not connected with a church, but we are
carrying out the principles of our faith.

This same premise is true for just about any area of business or service you can imagine — from opening a coffee shop
to decorating homes or launching a new retail product. It can
also be applied to an internal goal you may have for yourself. As
you grow with God, there is no telling the impact you will make
in your family and community. It starts with that first step of
faith, followed by a whole lot of prayer, trust, and focus. The
saying is true: "God equips you when He calls you."

Why did God do all of this in my life? I do not believe it was to own and operate a B&B. I am convinced that Tiffany Hill is not my legacy. No, the legacy of my journey is to inspire others to take a step of faith and follow what God has placed on your heart — that certain something that you cannot seem to shake or release. That thought, dream, or project that you try to release because it seems daunting, unrealistic, or too far-fetched! You never know; that might be the very thing that is His will for your life! Listen for the discernment of knowing you are going in the right direction. Yes, courage is abundant in the abstract. The difference between this little girl with a big 25-year-old dream is that I had a big God on my team to make it come true!

2.
Faith is Abundant in the Abstract

It is easy to proclaim your faith in the abstract, especially when all is well and life is good. Oftentimes discussions of religion or faith ensue either in a gathering of believers or among friends. Yes, many of us believe. But are we truly able to translate our faith into concrete steps? Are we able to take tangible action on that small voice we hear that keeps prodding us along on some thought or idea we cannot seem to shake? Faith becomes a bit trickier when you attempt to walk it. It is easy to talk the talk, but can you really walk the walk? How do you really KNOW? Just like courage is abundant in the abstract — so is faith.

We do a lot of things daily by faith. Maybe it happens over time as we become conditioned by the things we know will happen. If we do this, then that will occur. For example, you will go out to your car, put the key in the ignition, and the engine will start. You know that will occur because you have done it time and time again. You have faith in knowing the key will make the car start. If this, then that; cause and effect. Every day we step into the unknown, and yet we are assured of most outcomes based on the experiences we have grown to trust.

Now let's add God to the picture. Putting your faith in concrete terms with an intangible concept of faith in God is easier said than done. Putting all your trust and possibly even your life savings, like I did, into something you think you are being led to do is a huge step of faith. The only way to know, though, is to start — and along the way, you pray for discernment and clarity.

Faith is stepping out on a path that is unseen — it's having a knowing about something even though you cannot see it. There will surely be a lack of confidence since you do not have the comfort of knowing what will come next. Those clichés of "Jump and the lily pad will appear" or "Shoot for the moon; even if you miss, you'll land among the stars" are fun to hear, but when you are entering a dimension that is unknown and untested, it isn't entirely reassuring. To succeed, though, you must begin or you will remain frozen in your current circumstance.

Trusting God with Your Dream

How do you trust something that is invisible? How do you lay down everything you hope for and dreamed of doing for something you cannot see? Thank goodness these questions sent me on a path of discovery of how to trust God!

In this "show me" world it is hard to have faith in something intangible. In James we are told, "Grow closer to God and He will grow closer to you." It truly is that simple! It starts with a first step created by a desire to know more and grows over time. My time of spiritual preparation spanned seven years.

Many of my friends watched as my faith grew stronger and stronger. Several of us were actually seeking and growing together. But others were curious and skeptical of what they were seeing. One of my pastors once told me that as my faith grew, some of my friends would fall away. Interestingly, some of my dear, long-term friends inquired about how I developed my faith. They saw the metamorphosis of the street-smart, strong-willed, determined girl shifting in spirit. One friend said she wanted what I had, but did not know how to go about it. The answer is in the Bible in black and white…grow closer to God. It really is that simple!

How exactly do you go about growing closer to God? My suggestion is to become His student. Open that Bible and start learning. Don't be overwhelmed by all the different versions. They were all actually written to try to help people understand the Word. I found it overwhelming at first, but was thirsting to understand. One big mistake, in my opinion, is trying to read the Bible as you would a book. You open to Genesis, start reading, and get stuck in a dimension that might not be engaging to you. My suggestion would be to join a Bible study group or pick up a study guide at a local bookstore. You'll be surprised by how many intriguing thematic studies are in print — there's certainly something for every student of faith!

With so much to choose from, where do you start? I was fortunate to begin with a Disciple Study group at my church. Disciple is a great foundational program, but there are so many solid programs to choose from. Seek and you will find. I took five consecutive years of Disciple, a series of 36-week courses. And as I drew closer to God, He grew closer to me. I posed questions and the answers to my questions came from the pages of the Bible. Your answers will appear as you seek understanding. The more you seek, the more you will find.

Trust grows with experience, being in the Word, and discovering answers to questions. As you study the Word, leaning on Him for understanding, your mind opens up to the intangible. What a great and magnificent journey you will be on!

As I studied, I filled my world with the words and phrases that bolstered me:

Trust in the Lord
Lean on Him
Commit your ways to the Lord
The Lord directs the steps of the godly

The more I needed, the more I received. The more I sought, the more I grew. The more questions I had, the more answers were revealed. The more I discovered, the more dimension and meaning my life journey took on. God became my rock, and I was reminded once again that I could do anything as long as it was His will for my life that I was seeking. You must trust so that He can lead.

It all starts with the first step. There is a precious passage in Psalms declaring that God's word is a lamp unto our feet.

(Psalms 119:112) I've spent a great deal of time meditating on this promise. Often our fears are rooted in the unknown. For some, uncertainty is exciting. But for many, the immense mystery of where our dreams might lead us is enough to deter us from even beginning the journey. But take a moment to envision yourself standing on a dark road, gripping the handle of a lantern. Although you cannot see what's around you, your immediate path is clear, visible under a certain light. With each new step forward, the lamp also moves forward, leading you to a new illuminated area. Like this lamp-lit path, don't expect to know precisely in which direction your dream will take you — you'll risk disappointment if the road veers even slightly off course. Rather, focus on the end result, embrace the uncertainty, and release some control.

With your dream as the lamp that lights your feet, I promise you will find great joy in the journey. Leaning on God's Word as my lamp, I looked to the Bible for my direction, and began walking forward, one step at a time.

Leaning on Scriptures — the Journey

My faith was built on scripture, and it unfolded from abstract to concrete reality with the steps I took. At every point, I turned to scripture to lay the next step of my journey. Here's a look at my illuminated steps as the journey unfolded. Perhaps these passages of His Word will provide some illuminated insight for your path:

Initial Vision — Your Plan

*"If a voice is speaking to you now, do not look for reasons to ignore it.
There will always be reasons to stay where you are. It is faith that calls
you to move on. For we are God's workmen, created in Christ Jesus to do
good works which God prepared in advance for us to do." Ephesians 2:10*

Listen up! If something has been on your heart or in your
mind for years and you can't seem to shake it, reread the passage above. I was fortunate in my journey to have a good friend
finally connect the dots for me that my dream might just be
from God. If you sense that prodding, listen up and start stepping in the direction of your dreams!

Lesson of Patience

*"Trust in the Lord with all of your heart and be anxious for nothing."
Proverbs 3:5-6*

Getting answers to questions is wonderful, but trusting in
something that is invisible is not easy. We are told to trust in
the Lord with all our hearts. Let's get real; we are talking dollars
and cents here. Pouring all of your life savings into something
and trusting that you are doing the right thing and going in the
right direction — that if you "build it, they will come" — is easier said than done. There comes a time, though, that trusting is

all you can do. You commit your ways to the Lord and you walk together toward your dream. You BELIEVE. And when you believe, you start stepping in faith. You are in it and there is no going back. You are committed.

Transformation is not necessarily instantaneous. There's no winning lottery formula for an overnight success. Patience, perseverance, dedication, focus, and discipline are all words that described my seven years of transforming faith into reality. It may happen more quickly for your journey or it may be longer. No matter the length of time, be anxious for nothing. If this is, in fact, your God-ordained purpose, it will come to pass in the appointed time. My rear-view mirror perspective on my journey and the molding of my dream is abundantly clear.

Discerning Our Plans vs. His Plans

"In his heart, a man plans his course, the Lord determines his steps."
Proverbs 16:9

"The plans of the diligent lead surely to abundance."
Proverbs 21:15

"Commit your work to the Lord and your plans will be established."
Proverbs 16:3

Day after day and year after year, we go about making our plans, setting the course of action of what we think needs to be done. I urge you, though, to seek His guidance at each step. Be diligent in your work. It is not easy to carve out time to develop something new on the side. Unless you are born with that proverbial silver spoon, you are probably working to make a living. Stay focused with your eye on the end result — it may not happen overnight, but it will move forward in His time.

Seek and You Will Find — Building Confidence

> *"Ask and it will be given to you; seek and you will find; knock and the door will be opened to you. For everyone who asks, receives. Everyone who seeks, finds. And to everyone who knocks, the door will be opened."*
> *Matthew 7:7-8*

As you actively commit your plans to God, trust me that tangible things will occur. The key here is to recognize that these tangible milestones are actually from Him. Look for Him at work. Connections with people will be made which build bridges of assurance and confidence in your journey. Tune in to the prompts of the Holy Spirit and step in faith knowing that the path will illuminate in front of you.

As you step toward your dream, take action on the things that you are able to do and let God take care of the rest. The important part of this is to DO what you CAN do. You cannot expect God to do it all — you will have to do your part. One way to view this is that you are His foot soldier in the flesh.

I am continually amazed at how that book called the Bible will give you exactly what you need when you need it. That is why I believe it is called a living Bible. Here's a tangible example for you: As I was building the bed and breakfast, for some reason I came to the realization that it needed a cornerstone. What? That word had not passed through my consciousness ever before. Fortunately, a friend agreed to help me research what having a cornerstone even meant, where it was supposed to be placed, and what it should say. My charge was to show Christian hospitality to all people, meaning that I needed to be careful what I said so as to not deter folks from coming to Tiffany Hill. I initially thought the cornerstone would read "The B&B that God built," but the feeling poured over me that this particular phrase was a cop out for a dreamer who wanted to show Christian hospitality.

My last Disciple class was a parallel study of the Gospels. John is the last Gospel. Chapter 21 is the last chapter and there it was! John 21:12: "Come and have breakfast." I was so delighted to discover that passage that I immediately called one of my ministers and asked her if she knew of that scripture. When she said she did, I asked, "Why didn't you tell me?" Her answer tickles me to this day, "Well, I thought you already knew!" I had the perfect answer to my cornerstone predicament. Seek and you will find. Grow closer to Him and He will grow closer to you. The answers are there and they are waiting for you.

Recognize answered prayers!

"Ask and it will be given, seek and ye shall find."
Matthew 7:7

When the rubber started to hit the road and my dream began taking on more of a tangible reality, it became scary. I had been faithful in saving money, making plans, working on the design, and the timetable for my jump was closing in. You can imagine how sick to my stomach I was as the thought of leaving my steady paycheck came into focus. I prayed for inspiration and guidance. I needed to confirm that what I had been able to save was a solid number to jump with into my dream.

Then, the most amazing thing in happened. My participation in an industry conference reconnected me with a high school friend who had followed a similar path of building her dream bed and breakfast. Our reconnection after 30 years provided the confidence for me in concrete terms, knowing that my savings was sufficient. Then, she agreed to mentor me! Now I had someone who knew exactly what I was embarking on providing me assurance that I could succeed. An answered prayer indeed!

Sinking Moments

"I can do all things through Christ who strengthens me."
Philippians 4:13

This scripture has been the one I have leaned on the most. Often referred to as the "10 finger prayer" — making it easy to recall every time you need to remember that you can persevere through anything. I referred to this scripture not only when I stretched to do things I had never done before, but also when I felt my tasks were too numerous. Will you have sinking moments? Absolutely you will. We are all human. People and things will impact the way you think about your dream and your faith. Be careful to stay positive and know that you are growing with each situation you face — especially the ones that you think you cannot handle.

Stay Focused and Strong

"Faith is the assurance of things hoped for, the conviction of things not seen." Hebrews 11:1

Stand on it, believe it, and do not let others deter you. You have a knowing about the venture you are seeking that surpasses all understanding. Life is about choices — what we choose to think and what we allow to be verbalized. We become what we say and do. Be mindful about these forms of putting faith into action. You know the direction you are going — be sure you're always moving in the direction of your dreams. Keep in mind that if you stay still, nothing will happen. Stay positive and focused on your new reality that is unfolding in front of you.

It is your time!

> "To everything there is a season and a time for every purpose under the sun. There is a time to think our desires. There is a time to imagine our desires. Then there is a time to give our desires words. There is a time to do all the footwork necessary as we are listening to the Spirit for guidance. There comes a time to let our desires go with faith and give them to the Lord. Then there is the time we expect, when these same desires become real and are manifested in our lives. This is the harvest of our dreams."
> Ecclesiastes 3:1

These words held a whole new meaning for me when my faith was taking on dimension and things were beginning to happen left and right. When I was preliminarily approved for a $1 million loan, I could feel the scales sliding in the direction of the dream. It was so exciting! There comes a point when there are more reasons to walk into the dream than remain where you are — it's like a tipping point.

On one side of the scale, I felt like my old life and my career were meaningless, my savings plan was growing, and my confidence was firm. I was impressed that it was time to get on with life! The thrill of doing what you have been dreaming of overshadows all the fears and doubts that freeze you. It was getting harder and harder to juggle both my current dimension and the reality of my future. But fear of the unknown was still staring me in the eye.

Then it happened — the scales tipped! Out of left field, and without a moment's notice, I lost my job. God knew I was ready, even when I couldn't take the final step. He tipped the scale for me by orchestrating my departure from corporate America, along with a financial safety net called a severance package. It was time to choose to truly walk in faith, however risky that seemed, or to play it safe.

You will have what you need

> *"Therefore I tell you, do not worry about your life, what you will eat or drink; or about your body, what you will wear. Is not life more than food, and the body more than clothes? Look at the birds of the air; they do not sow or reap or store away in barns, and yet your heavenly Father feeds them. Are you not much more valuable than they? Can any one of you by worrying add a single hour to your life?"*
> Matthew 6:25-26

Trust in God to give you what you need when you need it. As my journey of faith unfolded after losing my job, another scripture in Exodus 16 was ever-present in my thoughts. In Exodus, the Israelites trusted God for provision of food, called manna, while they were in the wilderness. I felt like I, too, was in the wilderness with the security of my job no longer something I could stand on. Maybe my journey was amplified by the fact that I was a single woman! This was MY journey. There was no other person walking with me but my God.

Once again, a knowing poured over me that God would provide exactly what I would need. For the next two years, as the purchase of property took place and the bed and breakfast rose up from the ground, I would lean on this knowing of provision. When you are holding on to nothing but God — that is true faith. That's your honest test — fully relying on God.

The promise of manna (provision) became my rock of faith. Scripture tells us that without faith, it is impossible to please God. Faith, the substance of things hoped for, the evidence of things not seen. When we have faith, we stand on the knowledge that the Holy Spirit is at work even when we do not see evidence of it. When we have faith, we know we will receive what we have asked for. We don't waste our days worrying that the desires of our hearts will never come. Rather we wait in anticipation, knowing our good is already done. Where there is faith, there cannot be fear. With our faith, we know God is working on our behalf in the invisible. And what a relief that is! As He does that, prepare yourself for the fulfillment of your good in the visible. Stop fear in its tracks with a knowing that He is orchestrating the full scenario while you are doing your part.

With God, all things are possible

"For it is God who is at work in you, enabling you both to work for His good pleasure." Philippians 2:13

"Things impossible to men are possible with God." Luke 18:27

"With God, nothing is ever impossible." Luke 1:37

I was moving in the right direction. I did not know how to purchase land, but God did. I did not know how to build the B&B, but God did. I did not know how to maneuver the regulations, but God did. Walk by faith, not by sight . . . one step at a time.

Over the years, I had to put my faith into action. Little by little, step-by-step, I created a new reality based on faith. I leaned on Him to guide me, to build my confidence, and ultimately I laid my complete and full trust in what He was leading me to accomplish. Faith is the knowing of something even if you do not see it. When you stand on that knowing, you will realize that you are moving in the direction of God's will for your life.

Finish What You Set Out to Accomplish

"However, I consider my life worth nothing to me, if only I may finish the race and complete the task the Lord has given me." Acts 20:24

The most important thing you can do is fulfill why you are on this earth! Your life's mission should be to discern and complete the purpose of your life — your mission here. This is what God has placed you on this earth to do. Discerning what exactly that is, well that is the difficult part. But when you do, you have a singular focus and everything comes into view. Stay focused so you can complete what you set out to do.

Closing

In preparation for this book, I looked back on the collection of journals I penned over the span of ten years. One thing that consistently stood out in my writings was that the closer I walked with God, the more intense my journey became. This promise is revealed to us in James. It was almost as if He was leading me all along. Once I took the final step of faith, God took on all of my heavy lifting. I encourage you to spend time with Him in meditation, prayer, and conversation so that your confidence in knowing your dream is His will for your life will grow. After all, would you want anything other than His will?

God wants the very best for each and every one of us. He knows our desires and His plan for our lives is more magnificent than what we can imagine. If God is for us, who can be against us? Understand and acknowledge that He wants us to succeed. Acknowledge this Truth in your endeavors and see the will of God manifest. It is God's will that we accomplish the goals that we set for ourselves. When we are still and acknowledge Him, we are directed to the path that will lead to our greatest success. Indeed, it is God's will that we succeed.

Think about this for a moment. I was an unemployed single woman with a seven-month severance package. I obtained a million-dollar loan to build a bed and breakfast during the Great Recession, and then proceeded to build Tiffany Hill while drawing unemployment. That is faith and that is God!

Nineteen months after losing my job in corporate America, in the wee hours of the night, as I put the finishing touches on breakfast prep for the next morning, I crossed over from a B&B Wannabe to an actual Innkeeper. The development stage of the facility was now behind me. And it was good. The B&B was now open for business. I was in awe of what God had created. I prayed that I would remain calm and in His perfect peace so I could do what I was called to do — show hospitality to strangers, my guests. God had given me the desires of my heart, and it was an amazing journey.

Since then, so many guests have come and gone through the doors of Tiffany Hill. Oftentimes they will ask, "What is it?" What makes this place so special? What is the magic of Tiffany Hill? I know what they are sensing — it is God. He has put a stamp of approval on this place.

"For I know the plans I have for you" declares the Lord, plans to prosper you and not to harm you, plans to give you hope and a future." Jeremiah 29:11

God continues to bless the Bed & Breakfast on Tiffany Hill every day with the most incredible guests! Since the doors opened in 2009, I have prayed for blessings in the form of reservations. He has been faithful in sending the perfect people at the perfect time to bless this special place.

Faith is so very abundant in the abstract. It can also be SO VERY ABUNDANT in reality. I am grateful to see God at work in my life. The key is to be aware each and every day of the work He is doing.

3.
Dreams are Abundant in the Abstract

Before there was breakfast, there was a dream...

Did you ever daydream when you were young? I can remember staring out the windows in elementary school, completely lost in thought, while my teacher was doing her best to impart important information that would surely be included on the upcoming test. Research reveals that we daydream more when we are young, so it may have been commonplace for all of us. I can also remember daydreaming at work in my twenties, allowing my mind to wander when I was immersed in a task that I'd rather not be doing. At that stage of life, it was more of a mental escape from the work at hand — allowing pleasant thoughts about life or the future to float through the mind like a vacation to a tropical paradise.

Literally speaking, dreams are a series of thoughts, visions, or feelings that happen when you sleep. Dreams exist in the abstract without a physical or concrete existence. During my lifetime, the term "dream" has taken on more of an inspirational tone used to encourage people to pursue their goals. For example, "Believe in Your Dreams," "Dreams Do Come True," and "Follow Your Dreams." Dreams give us hope for something different than our current existence.

For many, dreams are abundant in the abstract! They jump from one thought to another in a split second. Every once in a while, a thought or dream might reoccur, whether while you are daydreaming or while you are asleep. You start formulating a mental picture of what your dream looks like, with you in the middle of it all. It's when a dream continues to reoccur that it has the possibility of turning into a passion and then a reality. It becomes not simply a passing thought, but something that you cannot seem to shake without surely taking some sort of action. It reoccurs over and over until you can't help but take that first step toward a new reality. That was the case with my B&B dream. It was not a choice — it became my passion, which I had to at least give a good try or I would forever live with the ultimate "what if."

A guest of the B&B once asked me to explain the difference between a dream and a goal. I am certainly no expert on the subject. My only expertise is gained through living a life where the seeds of a dream were planted, germinated over time, and with a lot of perseverance, dedication, and determination, my dream actually became a reality. Looking back, there was a progression from abstraction to reality where goals entered the picture. It started with a dream in the abstract. The dream then became a vision, an idea, a thought, concept, or object formed in my imagination. It was not real—it was something I could only see in my mind's eye and was not tangible.

The next stage was establishment of goals. Goals were created to achieve the desired results of what I had envisioned. With goals, tangible steps were established. It was at this stage that my dream shifted to become the object of my ambition, turning an abstract dream into concrete goals that created my new reality.

My hope for you is that your life has been filled with dreams and hopes achieved! Dreams come in all sizes, big and small. Some are easy to achieve, while others require more effort. Dreams give us hope for a better tomorrow, no matter what age we are. Dreaming can be so seductive, and so easy to postpone. None of them, though, will come to pass until you push the start button.

As a person of faith, I believe that many dreams are planted by God. The thought is that God designed humans to fulfill His purpose. He instills dreams and visions in us for a specific purpose. How many people do you know or have you heard of who have succeeded in a dream and then given all of the glory to God? They recognize that it was not all of their might, but His might that created their reality.

If you have been given a dream that you cannot seem to shake, remember, it might just be from above. Ecclesiastes 5:3 directs us to put effort into seeing our dreams come true. We are His instruments here on earth. As you stand at the beginning of the stepping-off point toward your dream or goal — what will become the new chapter of your life — you may not be able to clearly see how it will be used for His purpose. Trust in Him. If He is in it, it will most certainly become a reality. And when you look back, the path you followed will become clear. You might even become one of those people who give the glory to God!

Oh how I've sometimes wished that I had started earlier in life, that my dream of having a bed and breakfast had been realized five years sooner, etc. Looking back, I know that I was not ready spiritually or financially. My dream unfolded in the appointed time.

George Bernard Shaw once said, "Youth is wasted on the young." When I was younger, I was invincible, immortal, and fearless. My dream was abundant. It continued to be abundant for 25 years! Be careful, though. Time once spent can never be regained — use your time wisely. I feel so blessed to have lost my job in 2007, as I might have never hit the start button for my new reality — Tiffany Hill. God knew I was perfectly prepared and I credit Him for orchestrating my exit from corporate America.

How does one communicate to someone that life is short? We may have five, six, seven, maybe eight decades to live in our lifetime. The first two decades (ages 0 to 20) are dependent on others for basic necessities, and you have virtually no control or even understanding of what the big picture of life is all about. In decade three (your 20s) you are making your way into the world with possibly a college degree, finding a life partner, starting a career, making money, and establishing the course of your life. If you are a woman, you may be having children and starting to raise them to become responsible people in this world. There are a few people in their 20s and 30s who are fortunate to achieve their dreams early in life. Those who do typically have some wonderful talent that is discovered. But I would venture to say that most folks are more like I was when I was in my 20s — just ordinary people carving out their way in the world.

The seeds of my dream were planted in my third decade, but it seemed so far-fetched that it remained a pipe dream. So then comes decade four (the 30s). This decade is typically focused on raising the family started in the third decade. Or this decade may be focused on enhancing the career started earlier.

Right around decade five (your 40s) quite a few people experience a new awakening where they reflect on their life. For me, I felt like I was stuck in the dimension of earning a living to pay for my house, car, and other bills. I was just your average, ordinary person. How could I ever shift the flow of life from ordinary to extraordinary and live my dream? It was not until my sixth decade (my 50s) that things started to take shape spiritually and mentally.

Bottom line… there is no age limit to realizing your dream. I was in my mid-50s, single, and jobless when I opened the doors to my dream come true.

Thank goodness I took that first step toward my dream before I lost my job. Yes, I was propelled into shifting from courage is abundant to the reality of my dream because I lost my job. Luckily, I was ready and armed with all I needed to move forward in faith. I am so thankful that something happened to turn my existence from ordinary to extraordinary. What does it take to have the light bulb switch on for you? Don't wait too long to start and KNOW that it's never too late to pursue your dream. You can do it. It's time to follow the lamp you hold that illuminates the path before you. It just starts with that first step!

Maybe you have postponed your dream because you're waiting on the perfect time, the perfect situation, the perfect weight, the perfect degree, perfect savings, and the perfect connections to move forward. You must know that we are each responsible for what happens in our lives. If our dreams are to come true, it is up to us to make them happen. There may never be a perfect time; we are on His time.

Remember that anything is possible with God. If you have that knowing that surpasses all understanding, then you should believe it can happen. Choose this day to think positive thoughts about what you wish to accomplish. Affirm that you can do it. Today is the best day to choose to begin. Your dreams are just on the other side of putting your faith into action. Move in the direction of your dream, one step at a time. That is the only way you will get there.

You can do it! We just need to explore what it is you want to achieve and take the first step of faith. Now, it is time for you! Let's turn the page together and start unpacking your dream, vision, or goal.

Part II
It's All About You!
From Abstract to Reality

Hopefully, you have enjoyed reading about the journey to Tiffany Hill. My greatest hope is that by sharing my life's story, you will feel inspired to pick up your dream and move forward. Therefore, Part II of this book is all about you! Let's explore how you can use some or all of the tools I put in place to put you on the road to your Dream Come True, too!

Step 1: Laying the Foundation

What is YOUR dream, goal, or desire of your heart?

What are the deepest desires you cradle in your heart? Where do your passions lie? Dreams come in all shapes and sizes, so I'm not just talking to future innkeepers here. Perhaps your desire is to travel Europe, to become a master gardener, to lose 50 pounds, to achieve an early retirement, or to turn your hobby into a business. No matter where you are starting from, or where you wish to go, I am here to tell you that courage is abundant in the abstract — you need only take the first step toward your new reality. And that step is SO simple: Write it down!

My dream is to...

_____

_____

_____

_____

_____

_____

_____

_____

Or perhaps this is a better question for you: My goal is to...

_____

_____

_____

_____

_____

_____

_____

_____

Once it is written, you see it and can then articulate it. It becomes real. There it is in black and white. The first step is done. You have unearthed it.

What if you have multiple dreams? Who am I to deter you from multi-tasking? But, I have to say that it was difficult for me to focus my attention on my true destination while frittering my time on lesser goals. If your dream is a life destination, it might require all of your energy and time, so I would suggest you prioritize your goals and dreams and focus on the one that is the most important to you.

Hopefully we are in agreement with a singular destination in mind and you have that singular dream or goal written down.

Now comes the most important step in your journey. Please put down your pen to Stop, Pray, and Listen! This is the time to discern if what you wrote down is God's direction for you and His call on your life. You wouldn't want anything else now, would you?

This won't be the first time I suggest you put this book down so that you can focus on a pivotal point before moving forward. After all, you want to make sure that this is His will for your life.

My time of discernment took a year. At the end of that year, God told me I was going in the right direction. That was all I got! He did not say that my B&B dream would come true. He did not even tell me that what I was embarking on was correct. All I got was that I was heading in the right direction. From His affirmation, I knew I could continue forward with confidence that He was in it. I had a peaceful feeling about my direction once I had His assurance that I was moving in the path of my dream. I hope your affirmation comes quicker, but if it takes just as long, it is definitely worth the wait!

This is also the perfect time to speak to the concept of waiting. Waiting is an action verb! It is a choice. To "wait upon the Lord" is a daily decision. Some people think of waiting as doing nothing. I was questioned frequently from many people along the way: "Are you ever going to have a B&B?" "Will I see it in my lifetime?" WOW! Those were some tough words of doubt for this dreamer to hear. Choosing to wait is really tough when you are excited about moving forward. But wait you must! Until you have the stamp of approval from on high, you should just be still and view patience as a spiritual discipline.

How do you discern if this is the will of God? That is an age-old question many have addressed and tried to conquer. I spent a considerable amount of time trying to figure out what He wanted me to do. When I received direction from my minister to pray about it, I thought there had to be more to it than that. But, it is simple! Go to Him in prayer.

Personally, I prayed the same prayer for a solid year, day in and day out. I chose to wait until I knew that this was His direction for my life and not my personal willful direction. Laying down my will was the single most difficult thing I ever did, especially for this strong, German-stock woman. But I knew if I built my dream without it being from God, it would fail. To my delight, He gave me the desire of my heart to be an innkeeper. As time unfolded, my desire for innkeeping actually transitioned to a ministry of showing hospitality to strangers (and not just a fun thing to do in life). There was and is a tangible difference.

My prayer for you is that discernment of God's direction for you will be clear and in His time.

So now, once again, put this book down to Stop, Pray and Listen. Focus on this thought. Allow His communication to seep through the craziness of the messages you are bombarded with daily. When you have that peace of discernment you will know. Be sure to capture this moment. What did you hear? What did you feel? How did you know? Jot down your thoughts.

Date:

_____

_____

_____

_____

_____

_____

_____

Moving forward...

Congratulations! The foundation is set! You are moving in the direction of your dream or goal with God's stamp of approval. I am excited for you! With God all things are possible. Remember to go to Him with all things. Your discernment was not a one-stop, ah-ha moment, but rather the beginning of a magical journey. If you continue to engage Him, He will continue to guide and bless you.

That is not to say that you won't have challenges on this journey. There will be many! There have to be, or else we would not grow as individuals. Some people say that God will never give you more than you can handle. I believe the opposite is true! God will give you more than you think you can handle because He wants you to mature. With each obstacle you overcome or each milestone reached, you are growing with confidence into your new reality.

As a human in a real world of choices, chaos, and confusion, there will certainly be times when you think you might have bitten off too much. A poignant passage from Luke is appropriate here:

"For with God nothing is ever impossible and no word from God shall be without power or impossible of fulfillment." Luke 1:37

Believe you me, if God has sanctioned it and you believe, it will come to pass. You will most likely have a few twists and turns and sometimes feel lost or forgotten. Focus is key here. Don't lose focus of the destination in front of you. You have determined what it is you want to accomplish. You have prayed about it and discerned that this is what God has in store for you; you have a vision of your purpose in this world. Realize that He is bigger than you. With Him, all things are possible. If you believe, then fight for that belief and remain focused.

Step 1 is complete. You are of single purpose and have discernment that this is God's direction. Your foundation is laid and is solid.

Step 2: An important question — your driving force

Throughout my journey, there was one question that kept me focused and on track: What is the worst thing that can happen to you if you pursue your dream? Pick up your pen and answer that question before you move forward into the other tools we will explore. This is personal to you. You may know the answer instantly, or you may need a few days or even weeks to ponder. Please do not move forward until you have your answer. This will become an important motivator for you in achieving your dream. You will surely lean on this answer for inspiration many times at different stages of your journey.

Question: What is the worst thing that can happen to you if you pursue your dream?

Date:

_____

_____

_____

_____

_____

_____

Now that you have your answer to, you can face your fear head on. It may be a personal insecurity. It may be a financial situation. Or it may be something that confines your life.

Someone 15 years my junior asked me this question in the early stages of pursuing my dream. My single friend had recently up and quit her job in Atlanta, Georgia to focus on her dream. She wrote a business plan, successfully applied for a $60,000 loan, and was moving to Dallas, Texas, where she knew no one, in order to open a retail storefront.

Talk about impressed! To me — the "steady eddy" kind of gal with a paycheck coming every week, a nice home, and disposable income — her moxie was motivational! She said that when she had to answer the question about the worst thing that could happen, her answer was "filing bankruptcy and starting all over again." WOW! Impressive to say the least. I thought about that question for myself in the coming weeks. Filing bankruptcy was not an option for me — my father would roll over in his grave if I ever did that. But what WAS the worst thing that could happen to me?

It took some time for me to ponder this question and then finally, ding, ding, ding! My answer: Growing old, dying of natural causes, and looking back on my life to see that I never tried. How disappointing that would be. To have a dream that I could not shake for decades, talked about constantly to anyone who would listen, created an image of in my mind and on paper, and to have never taken that first step into my new reality. That truly WAS the worst thing that could happen to me! There were many moments along the path to Tiffany Hill when I needed to remember my answer to this question. There were times when I thought I was in over my head and wondered if I had better cut my losses. This very answer propelled me to the next level each time. The secret in succeeding is in trying. You have to do your best. And, there were moments in the journey that I was at peace in the knowledge that if it all stopped, I knew I had done my best. Failure is in not trying.

Hold onto your answer. You may need to lean on it from time to time. Let's move into exploring some tangible topics related to goal achievement and business development. When you are feeling low or have no clue where to turn for the next step, the answer you wrote will help keep you motivated along the way. Remember: What is the worst that could happen?

Step 3: Accountability Partners

After having this starry-eyed dream for so many years, there came a point where I knew I needed to do something. I needed to stop just thinking about my dream and take real action. Even if I made mistakes, even if I was wrong, I knew that I wouldn't feel fulfilled unless I did something.

It's time to put your dream in motion — to let it out into the universe by letting others know about it. You can choose to let a close circle know or you can cast a wider net — whatever you decide is best to keep you on track.

This step can actually be one of the hardest. Voicing your deepest desires or dreams leaves you a bit vulnerable. But I think you'll find yourself pleasantly surprised by how much support rolls in from those who care about you and your success. So many people want to encourage someone with a dream.

Find accountability partners who will listen with love, but also challenge you to succeed. These could be friends, family, local business owners, or clergy members. The important thing is that you get the idea out there and be open to the feedback of others.

List three to five people you want to hold you accountable. Keep in mind that they may not necessarily be your best friends, but rather the best people to keep you on track, people who can advise you, encourage you, and become a sounding board for you.

Bed & Breakfast on Tiffany Hill
Photo Gallery

The Grounds

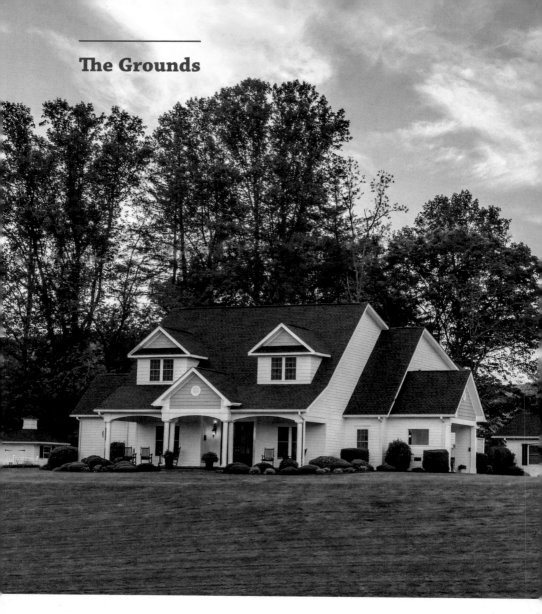

Clockwise from above: The Bed & Breakfast on Tiffany hill | An aerial view of Tiffany Hill, with the Adirondack Mountains visible in the distance | The Carriage House, with two suites — Lexington and Mountain Brook | The back dining patio, a beautiful setting to enjoy coffee or a glass of wine | The front porch, where guests can read a newspaper as they take in the fresh mountain air

Welcome to Tiffany Hill

Welcome to Tiffany Hill

The main entry hall

Main
House Suites

Madison

Beaufort

Natchez

Seaside

Charlottesville

Mountain Brook Suite

Carriage House Suites

Lexington Suite

**Breakfast on
Tiffany Hill**

On Tiffany Hill, a three-course gourmet breakfast is served every day.

Gardens of Tiffany Hill

My Accountability Partners:

1. _____
2. _____
3. _____
4. _____
5. _____

The individuals you identified above will become your most trusted advisors along your path. I even had several account-ability partners to help encourage me to write this book.

Initially, you will want to talk to each partner personally about your dream and ask them if they would mind encouraging you. Commit to a regular communication frequency with them so they know what to expect and can hold you accountable. You may communicate with them via email, talk to them individually, or invite them to dinner at milestone intervals of your journey. It is important that once you have invited them onto your team, you maintain communication. You might even ask them to reach out to you if they haven't heard from you about the journey for a while. Life is full, but your dream deserves focused energy and your accountability partners will insure that you continue to take positive steps toward the end result.

Step 4: Grow your Network

Your accountability partners are your inner circle, your strongest advocates who help you stay focused and on target. They are the ones you bounce ideas off of.

With them as your base, you may also want to grow your network from a marketing grassroots perspective. I found the more people who knew about my dream and its progress, the more encouragement I received. A wider network also gave me a wider perspective of opinions and ideas. My dream of having a B&B was not a proprietary, trademarked dream. Actually, there were many, many others who arrived at their B&B dream before I did. Maybe not a single woman who built it from the ground up, but people who achieved their destinies nonetheless. So the more people I met and shared my dream with, the more information I gained. Even if they were not familiar with the B&B industry, they would ask questions that helped me formulate my plan.

Personally, I needed a large group to keep me focused. I wanted everyone to ask me about my progress. So, in 1999 I sent my Dreambuilders letter to all of my friends, declaring with certainty that I would open a bed and breakfast in five years. In doing so, I created a larger network of accountability partners who continually queried me on the journey.

There are so many ways to communicate these days, from Facebook to texting! The more you communicate your dream or "talk the walk," the more support you will gain through encouragement from others. The other side of this is that the more you hear yourself talk about it, the more confident you will become in the new reality that awaits you. You will actually gain knowledge and understanding by letting it out to others and talking the walk.

When you are ready to cast the net of communications to a wider audience, what are three ways you can easily communicate to the masses? Think for a moment about whom you might need to communicate with and what would be the easiest way to deliver those communications.

Types of Communication Vehicles

1. _____

_____

2. _____

_____

3. _____

_____

Who would you want to know about your dream? Who might be your target audience? Who might lend a hand of support? Who can help you spread the word? Don't wait until you are ready to launch your dream to build your list. Today is the day! However it is easiest for you to start — from your collection of business cards to researching contacts in your industry — begin building your list today.

Excel spreadsheets have always been an easy way for me to manage tasks of long lists, but you might simply plug them into your phone. Today is the first day to start your list! You've already identified the very first people with your initial accountability partners.

Once you have a base of contacts, you will add new contacts every time you meet someone, every time you have an opportunity to research a different aspect of your dream, and every time there is a referral from someone new. You might build your list over six months or six years. Remember the $10,000 I collected from the Dreambuilders? That did not occur overnight. My initial start-up capital was gathered over a period of seven years.

Are you getting excited? Can you think of two people or 20 people you can add to your contacts? Now is a good time to put this book aside and focus. Open up a spreadsheet and start creating your list. Be sure to capture not only names but also email addresses, phone numbers, and maybe even mailing addresses. If the contact fits a category of assistance or knowledge, such as CPAs, lawyers, photographers, or architects, etc., you might make some notes now so you will remember that in the future.

Focus...

Step 5: Put Your Thoughts On Paper

If you have been pondering your dream and talking to others about your goals, I am certain that you have gathered thoughts or even tasks that need to be accomplished in order to arrive at your destination. At times, my mental task list was so overwhelming I could not find the starting point.

There is an easy exercise that will clear the clutter in your head — it's called Mind Dump. Start with a piece of blank paper and write down every single thing you can think of that would need to happen to make your dream come true. Think BIG, think small, think logistics, think time, think people. Let your mind wander and put it all on paper.

Be specific. What supplies will you need? Do you need a business plan? What start-up capital will you need? Do you need a marketing plan? Do you need a floor plan? Office furniture? What marketing materials, business cards, or other printed items will you need? There does not need to be any rhyme or reason to the list. Simply purge anything that comes to mind. Don't connect any dots at this point. Just do a free-form Mind Dump. Ask yourself what you need and and the doors of your dream will start to open. Release the clutter from your head. Whatever comes to mind, jot it down. Take the next 15 minutes and release.

What do you need to accomplish your dream?

Do you feel a sense of relief and lightness now? You should! Releasing all that has been swirling in your head should free you. There it is on paper. Concrete. You won't forget it.

Now, walk away from the list and from your focus for a bit; maybe for the rest of today or for a weekend or week. If something floats through your mind that is not on the list, come back to the list and jot it down. Do not worry about timetables or connecting the tasks, just write down anything you think you will need to achieve your goal or dream. My list had a lot of items, but I wasn't going to know where to start until I had that collection of things I thought needed to be accomplished written down in one place.

Step 6: Time to Put a Date on it!

When do you want to accomplish your dream? Through the Mind Dump exercise, you have an idea of what needs to be accomplished, so now you need to establish timetable. Be reasonable with yourself based on what your accomplishment list looks like, but at the same time come up with a target date of completion that will make you take action today. The size and scope of your goal will impact whether you put a date of a month from now or two years from now.

You never know what might trigger a timetable. My target date came about when one of my friends took a collection of her friends to Mexico, all expenses paid, for one of her milestone birthdays. What a great gift to us all! It made me ponder what I would want to do for my next milestone birthday, which was 2 1/2 years away. I had traveled just about everywhere I wanted to go, so travel was not the ticket for my celebration. Then it dawned on me! I wanted to have a pajama party at my Dream Come True, my very own bed and breakfast! How ridiculous and far-fetched it seemed at that moment.

Remember, I had been dreaming about this for decades! But NOW I had an end date — November 2009. I realized that I could not open the day before my projected date of the pajama party. After all, November would miss the summer travel season and we would be headed into a period of low revenue with the winter months ahead. In my mind, I needed to back the opening date up to Memorial Day Weekend. I estimated that it would take a year to build and took another guess that I should start looking for property at least six months before I projected the building start. Both of these guesses were based on my prior life experiences — but what matters for you is to put an end date on it. You need something to work toward and something that gives you a start date.

So on Labor Day 2007 I took the first real tangible step and hired a real estate agent in Western North Carolina to help me with the property search. Guess what? In November 2009 all the women who helped me on my journey to my Dream Come True celebrated with a pajama party on Tiffany Hill. I enjoyed an unforgettable birthday celebration!

As silly as this seems, my friend's milestone birthday celebration in Mexico created the timetable to make my dream concrete — and I knew I needed to get busy. When I went to Mexico in the spring of 2007, I had NO IDEA where the Bed & Breakfast on Tiffany Hill would even be built, but I knew it would be completed by summer of 2009

Your target date:

_____

Step 7: Pull it all together with a Project Plan

You have a list of what needs to get done and you also have a target date for your end result. Now, it's time to put it all together by outlining what needs to be accomplished when. You can start at your end date and work backwards, or you can start from today and move forward. The following pages are an example of what my project plan looked like for building and opening my B&B.

You may find you have to work through some bottlenecks in which too many things come together at once — just breathe and think it through. Talk it over with your accountability partners. Putting your tasks on a timeline will help organize the goal. Once you have it on paper in a linear fashion, you will see exactly what you need to do this week, this month, and this year to achieve your end result. Without this project plan, you could swirl around and around doing things that do not move you toward the direction of your dream.

Consider what tasks you excel at, and then decide if you might need help from other experts in areas that are not your strong points. You do not have to do everything on your own! For example, I am not a graphic artist, but I needed a logo. I found out that one of my neighbors loved creating logos, although it was not her professional career. We ended up trading services. She developed Tiffany Hill's logo and I created stained-glass windows for her home. We both got what we wanted and needed. Once again, it cost me very little.

Even if your dream or goal is not a business idea, you still need to break it down into achievable steps. Have milestone goals and develop a plan to get you to your desired result.

The next couple of sections of Part II: From Abstract to Reality address the financial aspects of a dream or goal. If you are not seeking to develop a business or a goal that requires capital, you already have what you need to move forward and start. You can skip ahead to Part III of the book. On the other hand, if you need money to fulfill your dream, then we need to explore what is needed for you to begin.

Step 8: Financial Aspects / Start-up Capital

As the pieces of your project become more concrete in your mind, I am sure that finances have started to creep into your thoughts. You have made lists of things you will need, from printed materials to furniture. Don't get overwhelmed. At this point, you are still planning. You may not even have spent a dime! Planning costs you nothing but your time.

It is now time to start pulling together the financial piece of your plan. You know the elements that will incur costs, so now you have to put a dollar amount on what you think you will require. Your estimates need to be reasonable, so you may need to place calls to experts, research over the Internet, or simply take your best educated guess. Here is what I projected as start up capital for the B&B back in 2007 (following page).

When I was on the other side of the dream, living my new reality, was this projection 100 percent accurate? No — but it did help guide me along the way. Once you write it down, you have an idea of what you will need to get started.

So, do you have all the monetary resources to fulfill your goal? If so, congratulations! You are on your way! If not, then we need to explore how you will obtain the financial support to make your dream come true. There are many ways to obtain financing. I cannot pretend to be an expert in this area because I am not. But I can share a few thoughts to get you started.

Sample for Initial Startup Capital

Selena Enterprises, LLC

Purchase Cost		Down Payment	$199,000
Cash Invested	20%	Monthly Payment	$5,374.65
Financing	$796,000	6.50%	25 years

Startup Operating Expenses		Business Development Costs	
Corporate Setup	1200	Start-up Operating Costs	131,300
Licensing	500	Land (7 Acres)	245,000
Capital Equipment	2,000	Building	750,000
Furnishings	75,000	**Total**	$1,126,300
Supplies	500		
Pantry Stock	600	**Security and Collateral for Loan Proposal**	
Advertising/Marketing	4,000	Real Estate	199,000
Linens	1,500	Other Collateral	250,000
Utility Deposits	1,000	**Total**	$449,000
Website	20,000		
Working Capital	25,000		
Total Startup Expenses	**$131,300**		

Sources of Capital	
Owner's Equity	320,000
Bank Loans	796,000
Other Investors	10,000
Total Source of Funds	**$1,126,000**

The first place I looked for financial support was myself. I took stock of what I had in savings, what I was earning, and what I was spending — and then I started to make decisions on what was important to me. Was it really necessary to drive a new car every other year, or should I put that money in the bank so it could earn interest?

I also needed what money I was able to save to work harder for me. I practiced Frugal is Fun for seven years, living with a paycheck-to-paycheck mentality while my earnings were being channeled into mutual funds to help grow what I was able to save. Spend less, earn more, and save every penny. It was exciting to watch my nest egg grow without having to work harder!

Personal savings was a part of what I needed, but this did not cover the entire start-up projection. The Dreambuilder Fund was amazing from the perspective of how many encouragers came aboard to support this dreamer, but their $100 deposits only scratched the surface of the million-plus needed for my project.

The next area to consider exploring is family and friends — but tread lightly. This can get tricky and you don't want to risk your relationships for money. My family was not in a financial position to help and I did not want to risk my friendships by seeking financial support. Moving along the chain of financial assistance might be grants, angel investors, and other financial avenues specific to your dream. You hear of all kinds of financial investors, even those on television. Explore any that make sense to you, but be careful to keep on eye on what they may want in exchange for their financial investment.

The traditional way of obtaining financial support is to go to a bank. After all, they have all the money, right? You will need more than the dream statement, project plan, and start-up capital projection you have pulled together for them to take you seriously, though. Their willingness to lend you money will be based on what your financial projections will be and their risk assessment of your endeavor. You will need to mentally get inside your daily operations and pull together a 1-year, 3-year, 5-year projection. For reference, here is what was presented for my request for a $1 million loan:

Sample Projection List

Short Term Goals

- A double digit growth rate for successive years
- Focus on repeat traffic for at least 30%
- Reduce variable costs per guests
- Continue to decrease the fixed cost
- Establish business presence for Selena's Glass Room

Three-Year Goals

- 50% occupancy
- Addition of a two-bedroom cottage

Five-year goals

- 70% occupancy
- Increase room rate and reduce occupancy rate
- Streamlined operations
- Ability to accelerate retirement of debt

Same 3-Year Cash Flow Projections

Cash Receipts	Year 1	Year 2	Year 3
Number of rooms	5	5	5
Cash Sales	$122,442	$153,411	$187,124
Estimated Occupancy	36%	45%	50%
Estimated Room Nights	662	829	922
Gift Shop Income	$14,050	$15,600	$16,650
Event Room Rental	$5,000	$5,000	$5,000
Total Cash Receipts	$142,154	$174,841	$209,696
Total Cash Available (before cash out)	$169,173	$223,893	$283,300
Cash Paid Out			
Debt Service	$68,028	$68,028	$68,028
Advertising	$3,673	$4,602	$5,614
Food	$9,266	$11,610	$12,912
Salary/Management Fee	$3,600	$3,600	$3,600
Gas	$3,061	$3,835	$4,678
Telephone	$3,420	$3,420	$3,420
Electric	$6,122	$7,671	$9,356
Water and Sewer	$0	$0	$0
Supplies	$2,449	$3,068	$3,742
Maintenance	$1,837	$2,301	$2,807
Outside Services	$3,000	$3,000	$3,000
Vehicle Insurance and Repairs	$1,200	$1,200	$1,200
Accounting and Legal	$900	$900	$900
Bank/Merchant Services	$3,061	$3,835	$4,678
Property Insurance	$3,000	$3,000	$3,000
Real Estate Taxes	$4,296	$4,296	$4,296
Occupancy Tax	$4,898	$6,136	$7,485
Sales Tax	$8,230	$10,191	$12,282
Association Fees	$600	$600	$600
Internet Service	$3,600	$3,600	$3,600
Pest Control	$900	$900	$900
Total Cash Paid Out	$135,140	$145,794	$156,098
Cash Position (End of Year)	$34,033	$78,100	$127,202

Same 3 Year Cash Flow Projections

	Pre-Startup EST	Jun-09	Jul-09	Aug-09	Sep-09
Cash on Hand (beginning of month)	25,000	25,000	26,582	28,163	29,745

Cash Receipts

	Pre-Startup EST	Jun-09	Jul-09	Aug-09	Sep-09
Number of Rooms		5	5	5	5
Cash Sales		$12,904	$12,904	$12,904	$14,338
Estimated Occupancy		45%	45%	45%	50%
Estimated Room Nights		70	70	70	78
Gift Shop Income		$500	$500	$500	$750
Event Room Rental		$500	$500	$500	$500
TOTAL CASH RECEIPTS	0	13,474	13,474	13,474	15,166
Total Cash Available (before cash out)	25,000	38,474	40,056	41,637	44,911

Cash Paid Out

	Pre-Startup EST	Jun-09	Jul-09	Aug-09	Sep-09
Debt Service		$5,669	$5,669	$5,669	$5,669
Advertising		$387	$387	$387	$430
Food		$977	$977	$977	$1,085
Salary/Management Fee		$300	$300	$300	$300
Gas		$323	$323	$323	$358
Telephone		$285	$285	$285	$285
Electric		$645	$645	$645	$717
Water & Sewer		$0	$0	$0	$0
Supplies (office & oper.)		$258	$258	$258	$287
Repairs & maintenance		$194	$194	$194	$215
Outside services		$0	$0	$0	$250
Vehicle/Insurance/Repairs		$100	$100	$100	$100
Accounting & legal		$75	$75	$75	$75
Bank/Merchant Services		$323	$323	$323	$358
Property Insurance		$250	$250	$250	$250
Real Estate Taxes		$358	$358	$358	$358
Occupancy Tax		$516	$516	$516	$574
Sales Tax		$808	$808	$808	$910
Association Fees		$50	$50	$50	$50
Internet Services		$300	$300	$300	$300
Pest Control		$75	$75	$75	$75

	Pre-Startup EST	Jun-09	Jul-09	Aug-09	Sep-09
Subtotal	0	11,892	11,892	11,892	12,646
Capital Improvements*					
Capital purchases*					
Reserve and/or Escrow*					
Total Cash Paid Out	0	11,892	11,892	11,892	12,646
Cash Position (end of month)	25,000	26,582	28,163	29,745	32,265

Oct-09	Nov-09	Dec-09	Jan-10	Feb-10	Mar-10	Apr-10	May-10	Total Item EST
32,265	37,864	40,343	41,845	35,976	31,107	27,331	26,008	27,018

Oct-09	Nov-09	Dec-09	Jan-10	Feb-10	Mar-10	Apr-10	May-10	Total Item EST
5	5	5	5	5	5	5	5	
$17,205	$11,470	$7,169	$2,868	$4,301	$5,735	$8,603	$12,044	$122,442
60%	40%	25%	10%	15%	20%	30%	42%	36%
93	62	39	16	23	31	47	65	662
$2,000	$3,000	$5,000	$200	$250	$400	$450	$500	$14,050
$500	$500	$500			$500	$500	$500	$5,000
19,299	14,532	12,208	3,083	4,575	6,166	9,099	12,609	142,154
51,563	52,397	52,551	44,928	40,550	37,273	36,431	38,617	169,173

Oct-09	Nov-09	Dec-09	Jan-10	Feb-10	Mar-10	Apr-10	May-10	Total Item EST
$5,669	$5,669	$5,669	$5,669	$5,669	$5,669	$5,669	$5,669	$68,028
$516	$344	$215	$86	$129	$172	$258	$361	$3,673
$1,302	$868	$543	$217	$326	$434	$651	$911	$9,266
$300	$300	$300	$300	$300	$300	$300	$300	$3,600
$430	$287	$179	$72	$108	$143	$215	$301	$3,061
$285	$285	$285	$285	$285	$285	$285	$285	$3,420
$860	$574	$358	$143	$215	$287	$430	$602	$6,122
$0	$0	$0	$0	$0	$0	$0	$0	$0
$344	$229	$143	$57	$86	$115	$172	$241	$2,449
$258	$172	$108	$43	$65	$86	$129	$181	$1,837
$250	$500	$500	$500	$500	$500	$0	$0	$3,000
$100	$100	$100	$100	$100	$100	$100	$100	$1,200
$75	$75	$75	$75	$75	$75	$75	$75	$900
$430	$287	$179	$72	$108	$143	$215	$301	$3,061
$250	$250	$250	$250	$250	$250	$250	$250	$3,000
$358	$358	$358	$358	$358	$358	$358	$358	$4,296
$688	$459	$287	$115	$172	$229	$344	$482	$4,898
$1,158	$872	$732	$185	$274	$370	$546	$757	$8,230
$50	$50	$50	$50	$50	$50	$50	$50	$600
$300	$300	$300	$300	$300	$300	$300	$300	$3,600
$75	$75	$75	$75	$75	$75	$75	$75	$900

Oct-09	Nov-09	Dec-09	Jan-10	Feb-10	Mar-10	Apr-10	May-10	Total Item EST
13,699	12,053	10,707	8,952	9,444	9,942	10,422	11,599	135,140
13,699	12,053	10,707	8,952	9,444	9,942	10,422	11,599	135,140
37,864	40,343	41,845	35,976	31,107	27,331	26,008	27,018	34,033

Remember, you are making projections — but they need to be reasonable. You can certainly reach out to people who have accomplished similar goals and ask for their projections. The Internet is also a great resource these days. Put a number to each line item you think will cost you something, as well as what you think will be your revenue projections. The bank will review these charts to check for reasonableness. They will be evaluating based on whether you can cover your expenses and grow the business over time.

Step 9: Marketing Plan

You have a great idea, which you firmly believe will be well received in the marketplace. For some, transitioning from the initial idea or concept to people actually spending their money on what you have created is a nightmare. If you are developing a new invention or product, it is more challenging than if you are replicating something already in the marketplace. It is so much easier to walk in the footsteps of others. For example, I wanted to build a B&B. There are thousands of others who own existing B&Bs and I was able to reach out to them to inquire about the aspects of operation. Thousands of existing B&B owners purchased their business as a B&B. Others took on a project of converting a historic building to turn it into a B&B. None of these paths were ones I wanted to follow. There were a few others who actually built their own B&Bs, but I could not find any B&B that was built by a single woman, or even a single man, for that matter.

Of the ones that had been purposely designed and built as B&Bs, I found one whose owner I was fortunate to have mentor me. The point is that you can learn from others. Most people are very willing to share their experience and are happy someone asked. They are on the other side of their dream come true. Don't be afraid to ask.

Now let's talk Marketing. Marketing can be incredibly daunting, so it's helpful to break it down. There are several components of marketing. It starts with a solid product or service and ends with distribution and sales. As you begin to think about marketing, start with the end in mind. Knowing your potential audience is key. Paint a picture of who you think would be interested in your product. What do they look like? What would they read? Where do they shop? How old are they? Are they male or female or both? What do they like to do? How much do they earn? What is their education level?

Some of these questions are fairly easy to answer initially. When I was dreaming of Tiffany Hill, I thought my audience would be predominantly Baby Boomers with some college and a disposable income above $75,000. After being open for five years, we do see this segment, but have been surprised to also discover that almost a third of our guests are professionals under 30 years old who enjoy hiking and biking in the forests adjacent to where we are located. What I am hoping to convey is that you can project who your audience might be so that you can initiate marketing efforts, but be nimble enough to shift your strategies as you roll out.

Large companies spend millions of dollars in market research — everything from focus groups to surveys to brand sampling. In all probability, you do not have that capacity. You will still need to paint a picture and go for it! Once you have an idea in your mind of who your audience is, you can then start to develop the marketing materials that will appeal to them.

The following chart provides a marketing framework:

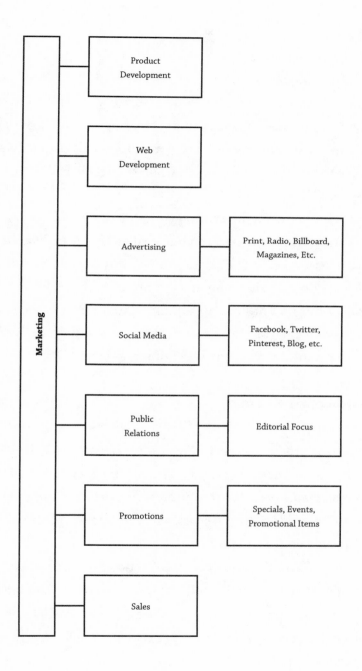

Oftentimes I hear of people overwhelmed by marketing. When we talk about why it is so overwhelming, their answer is typically sales. It takes a certain personality to make cold calls! When you believe in what you are creating, though, those cold calls are easy to do and vital to your success. Everyone has the ability to become a salesperson when they truly believe in what they are selling.

Each one of the marketing components in this chart is as important to the success of your goal as the next. Even if you have a natural flair for sales, you will not be able to sell anything without having a good solid product. If you have a solid product but do not have appealing collateral materials, you do not have what you need to convey your product. Let's touch more specifically on each aspect of marketing:

Product or Service

Whatever product or service you offer needs to be the best it can be! Is it something people need or want? What do you think is a reasonable price for your product or service? Shopping other similar products or categories in your marketplace will help you decide your price point.

On Tiffany Hill, our guests often comment that we have thought of every detail for their comfort — from Kuerig beverage centers to piped-in music to black makeup washcloths. This did not happen overnight or by accident. I collected research from other properties over the course of 25 years so that the product I offered would be the best it could be. Yours needs to be the best in your category, too!

Website

In this day and age, most everyone needs a website to represent their product. Websites are simply another form of advertising. Even if it is a static display with information on how to contact you, a website is essential. If anyone wants to know anything about anything, they most likely will Google it! There are many ways to create a website without breaking the bank. Again, your graphic artist will probably be able to help you here or give you a referral to someone who can assist with developing a site.

The following information should give you a foundation for the elements of a website. As a non-technical person who worked in a technical company most of my life, I know there are very few technical people who will take the time to convert the technical jargon into layperson terms. My goal here is to simply take a bit of mystery out of web development — and hopefully inspire you to get you started.

A few elements of a website

URL | Uniform Resource Locator. This is your website's address on the World Wide Web. A URL is the fundamental network identification for any resource connected to the web. For Tiffany Hill, it looks like this:

http://www.bbontiffanyhill.com/rooms.htm

There are more than one hundred million websites on the Internet — all of which have a unique domain (hostname above) name. The domain name you choose should reflect your product or company name. You can check the availability of your desired domain name and secure it from a registrar or the current owner.

Go to an domain registrar and web hosting company online. Some popular options are GoDaddy, Network Solutions, Register.com, and Wild West. These websites will have a field to check availability of any given domain. If your desired domain is available, you can use any of the above sites to register the domain in your name. Even if your dream is years away, if the domain name is available now, go ahead and buy it. You don't have to use it until you are ready, and it will help you cement your dream.

Web Host | A web host is basically a company that has many computers connected to the Internet. When you place your web pages on their computers, everyone in the world will be able to connect to it and see your pages. You will need to sign up for an account with a web host so that your website has a home. If getting a domain name is like getting a business name for your company, getting a web hosting account is comparable to renting space for your business on the World Wide Web.

Web Design | There are several directions you can go in designing a website. You can try to do it yourself or hire a website designer. My advice is that if you are not technically oriented, this might be one of those areas to seek the help of someone who is. Websites are not that expensive these days and you can do some research, either through friends or by surfing the net for websites you like, to get ideas. At the bottom of the home page for most sites will be the web designer information.

Before you hire a designer though, make sure you know what you want to accomplish with your site. Is it going to be a static information webpage or will it have an ecommerce element? How many pages do you need? What is your content for each page? What color palette do you want to use? This is really easy! Start surfing the net and see what appeals to you. These sites don't have to be in your same industry, but you will want to make sure you review what your competitors have online as well. Start collecting sites that you like so that you can give the web designer some ideas of where to start.

When I was working with my designer, I sketched out a page for each of the web pages I thought I needed. Then we collaborated on the layout and content. Having an idea what you want upfront is critical to the end result. A bit of research on your part will go a long way in communicating what you are looking for and save money in the long run.

The home page of your website is your calling card and typically your landing page. This is the first introduction to your product or service. Remember the old saying, "You never get a second chance to make a first impression?" Be sure to put your best foot forward. Keep in mind that people are time-deprived these days, with so much information coming at them. We are all SO connected. Your home page should clearly convey in a matter of seconds who you are and what you offer. Include contact information. Use a combination of photographs and text. Try to avoid too much reading material. You have only seconds to make that first impression, so capture their attention and make them want more.

Ecommerce | If you want to sell your product or service online, another essential element of your website will be Ecommerce. Don't think you need to build the shopping cart system on your own. Thankfully there are many programs that are already online to choose from. For a fee, you can plug in an ecommerce element to your site.

For Tiffany Hill, I needed a reservation system. My web developer did not have to create that for me. I found several B&B reservation systems to choose from. Once I decided on which reservation system I wanted to use, my web designer simply added a portal for the ecommerce element and we were done. It was that easy and will be for you as well.

As your website is finalized, go back to your Accountability Partners or your first customers and ask for their opinion. In other words, test it on them. Also remember to inquire of your first customers for product or service reviews and have those incorporated into your site. Nothing speaks more loudly to prospective customers than reviews.

Advertising Print Materials

You have a great product; don't overlook the need for a brand identity. How do you want your product portrayed? What colors will you use, what lettering, what visuals? Will it be whimsical or will it be more serious? Your brand is your visual representation of your product. When developing the logo for Tiffany Hill, we worked for months to create the right look and feel. Seek out a graphic designer and get started. If you don't know how to find a graphic artist, ask your accountability partners — they may know someone who can assist you.

Once you have a brand identity, you can decide which collateral materials you need to support your sales team (which may be a team of one — yourself — to start). Business cards are a universal need. These are literally your calling card. But what else do you need? What appeals to your audience and what are the best vehicles to communicate with them? In the B&B industry, we have rack cards in our tourism offices and welcome centers — so that is a given.

In my previous life in the lottery industry, our top advertising medium was billboards along the highways to communicate jackpot awareness. You will need to decide what is right for your product. Then your graphic artist can assist with layouts of whatever you have decided will be needed for you to market your business venture. Be careful not to create too much or spend an excessive amount of money upfront. In all likelihood your materials will evolve, so get just what you need for now to get started. A good source of low-cost printing is VistaPrint.com. You might also consider an in-kind trade with a local printing company where you offer your product or service for their print services.

Mass Advertising

You want to spread the word about your new service or product, so of course advertising is needed, right? Maybe, but be careful here. There are all sorts of mediums for advertising, from newspapers to magazines, billboards to television. Paid advertising is not inexpensive. You may not have the budget initially to support a paid advertising campaign. Know that advertisers also entertain in-kind trade for their services. You can possibly negotiate a reduced price for advertising or maybe even get advertising for free. If you don't ask, you will never know.

Keep in mind that you have created a solid and wonderful product or service. The best form of advertising is word of mouth! Getting your product in the hands of people who will talk about it with others is another form of advertising. Now is the time to go to the list of contacts you have been gathering. Next, look at categories of businesses or people who might be interested in your offering. For example, one B&B I know used to give free nights to hairdressers, knowing they would share their experience with their customers.

As customers use your product or service, ask them to share their experience with others by placing a review on your website. You may even offer an incentive initially to help start your reviews. In this day and age, people want to read about other customers' experiences before they make a decision to buy a product or service.

Social Media

Social media runs the gamut, from Facebook — with over 1.5 billion users — to Twitter, Instagram, Pinterest, blogging, and so on. Social media is an effective, low-cost way to engage the masses. In the B&B industry, I find that it keeps my existing customers engaged on an emotional level with what is happening at my place of business but does not create new customers.

Whether social media cultivates customers or not, you need to be in the game. Creating a Facebook page for your business is free and a good place to start. It would be good for you to dabble in each of the social media mediums to see what results. You might land on a wonderful way to advertising your business and gain new customers. I would caution you to keep a keen eye on results. Analyze the amount of time spent via social media as compared to other advertising outlets.

Public Relations (PR)

From your local newspaper to national publications, writers are always looking for fresh story lines. Your initial product launch, store opening, or new service offering is a worthy story in at least your local press. Reach out to them and let them know what you are doing. You never know, sometimes those local stories are picked up over the press wire service for a broader reach.

Create and maintain a list of press contacts to whom you can send information as you release new aspects of your dream or as you reach milestones in product sales or significant anniversaries. If you do not share what you are doing, your dream will remain a well-kept secret — and what's the fun in that? You have to be the biggest cheerleader and promoter of your dream. In the midst of producing your product, paying bills, dealing with operational issues, and maneuvering the challenges of a start-up business, you must carve out time to get the word out there or no one will know it exists.

The public relation area of marketing could very well become your best return of investment of your time. But it does take time. One good public relations hit in a regional or national publication can propel you into new heights for product demand.

Promotions

You have a great product, your collateral materials are underway, and you've started creating your website. Now you should consider how you spread the word by promoting your product. You need it seen. This is called brand awareness.

Think of the lemonade stand you opened when you were young. You could pitch a tent in your front yard and all who pass by would be introduced to your product or service. But what if there was a way to get in front of a lot of people who were looking for a product or service like yours who didn't happen to stroll by?

Tradeshows or markets are ideal for showcasing certain products or services. You will need to research the best fit for you. Talking about your wares in front of a lot of people will sharpen your presentation and ultimately refine your product position.

Another aspect of promotion that entices buyers is special discounts. You want customers to sample your service, like it, and want more of it. As a prospective customer, you may not be willing to pay full price for some unknown product, so discounting is a wonderful way to entice future fans. Don't be afraid to create specials to make your way into the marketplace. Large corporations do this all the time when they launch a new product. Just be careful not to make your promotional offer so low that you do not recoup your expenses and make a little profit. Start small with your special offers, knowing that you can support the demand. Once you have your feet on the ground and have a sufficient supply, don't be afraid to mass promote your product or service through discount sellers like Groupon, Living Social, or Daily Deals. All of these have mass distribution lists of purchasers who are looking for a deal. It's a great way to have people sample your product. Once you have happy customers, they will help spread the word as well.

Sales

There is an age-old organizational debate as to whether sales and distribution belong under marketing or as a separate entity. Since you are most likely wearing all the hats of your organization, we will set that debate aside and keep it with marketing.

Your product is wonderful! You have developed a brand identity that best represents your new business. You have amazing collateral materials to convey your new product or service. A website exists so that potential buyers can find out more information and locate you when they make their decision to purchase. You have succeeded in getting the word out that you exist in the marketplace through promotions or PR. Great! Now you have to sell, sell, sell.

Yes, you need to pick up the phone or go door-to-door, literally or figuratively, and ask for the sale. You believe in your product, don't you? You know your target audience, so find them and ask them to purchase your product. What good is a shelf full of widgets if you cannot exchange them for money? If you believe in what you are doing, this will not be as hard as you think.

Personally, I talk about the B&B with every person I come in contact with — and I have for years. People knew about my dream long before I ever settled on a location to build. Believe it or not, this created pent-up demand. Everyone I came in contact with could very well be my next guest — or they may know someone who will become my next guest.

A great way to get started in sales is by developing a 30-second elevator commercial. This is a short introductory sales pitch that should pack a punch. Think about the length of an elevator ride — 30 seconds, more or less. You want your speech to be memorable and define what you do. I use my elevator speech every time I meet someone new, and have since this dream of mine came into view. I simply changed my description to either "am building," "looking to open," or "owner of." Here's what I mean:

Hello, my name is Selena Einwechter, and I own the Bed & Breakfast on Tiffany Hill near Asheville, North Carolina, where you can have breakfast at Tiffany's.

From that brief introduction, they know I own a B&B in North Carolina and they will remember breakfast at Tiffany's, each of which are great Google words and phrases. So start today in creating your first sales pitch — your 30-second elevator commercial. It's never too early to start making an impression on who might become your next customer.

Speaking of customers, they fall into two categories: existing and new. Keep your existing customers happy! Once you have a customer, it is less expensive to keep them happy and engaged than to cultivate new customers. You will need to balance your time in order to devote time to existing customers. Keeping customers engaged these days is so much easier than ever before. Facebook and newsletter services like Constant Contact are easy to navigate once you have them set up. These are great tools to engage customers you already have.

New customers will come from all the other marketing tools we have touched on. Yes, you will wear a lot of hats when it comes to marketing! You will have to keep a lot of balls in the air at the same time. It is critically important, though, to always keep an eye on your product. Your product is the single most important aspect of your business. If your product quality is compromised, everything else will suffer.

For the purposes of a marketing plan, the following will give you an idea of what a market analysis and a 3-year marketing plan looked like for the business plan I submitted for Tiffany Hill. What the lender is trying to glean from your proposal is whether you've evaluated your market and whether your plan is financially viable.

Sample Market Analysis

The most successful market location for a bed & breakfast should include the following characteristics:

Location

- 40,000 to 100,000 population
- 2 to 4 hours of urban areas
- Tourism/Travel destination
- Within 30 minutes of a regional airport
- College town
- Independent restaurants
- Quaint retail area
- Regional hospital
- Other B&Bs in area

Other Bed & Breakfast Facilities

Henderson County, North Carolina currently has approximately 20 B&Bs. Most of these represent historic village properties. It has never been my intent to be the only B&B in a town. The fact that the area can sustain multiple B&Bs creates a healthy, competitive, and cooperative environment. It also is an opportunity to create product differentiation by becoming the most desired location in the marketplace. Within Henderson County is the newly incorporated Mills River area. One edge of distinction mentioned earlier is there are no other lodging facility in this new municipality. Becoming the first in this developing town is certainly getting in on the ground floor.

Sample 3-Year Marketing Plan

Year 1

- B&B Association member and advertising
- Establish Internet placement
- Chamber of Commerce
- By word-of-mouth
- Direct mail semi-annual campaigns
- Postcards
- Friends & family - Any friend of yours is a friend of mine
- Create promotional packages
- Frequent Pillow Program
- Fill the Rooms campaign (Mayor/Governor/Ministers/ Doctors)
- Business to business development with corporate rates
- Implement annual open house
- Special occasion venue for local community
- Apply to Select Registry
- Build strategic relationships with local college business offices

Year 2

- Annual calendar
- Learning Retreats
- Herb gardening
- Yoga
- Church retreats
- Scrapbooking
- Antiques & collections
- Cooking classes
- Cottage industry upstarts
    - Craft show & open house
    - Target advertising in 5 hour radius metro areas
- Establish presence in print media & on-line news sites
    - *Southern Living*
    - *Inn Traveler*
    - ajc.com/travel

Year 3

- Establish Inn-to-Inn reciprocal travel agreements
- Target small reunions
- "Big Chill" reunions

Step 10: Business Plan

Classically speaking, a business plan is a collection of documents that outline the proposed business goals and initiatives to achieve those goals. Banks use your business plan to evaluate the financial feasibility of you accomplishing your end result. They will apply their internal calculations to determine if you are a solid credit risk. Of course the more financial backing you are looking to attain, the more information they will likely want from you. The development of the plan will force you to evaluate the feasibility of your business venture. In other words, it will make you "think before you jump" so that you can step more assuredly.

The other primary reason for developing a business plan is to create a roadmap for you to follow internally. It helps organize your thoughts as you are considering all the aspects of your business. You will want to address all stages of your business, from start-up through your exit strategy.

Whew — that sounds like a lot. But do not get overwhelmed! You do not have to have a degree in business to write a stellar business plan. In fact, many entrepreneurs never attend college.

When I embarked on developing the business plan for Selena Enterprises, LLC, I took lots of courses, bought numerous books on the subject, and spent thousands of dollars trying to educate myself on how to write a plan. Then one day I discovered a free Microsoft business plan template online. Bingo!

Initially, that template had nothing to do with what I wanted to accomplish, but it did provide a start, or rather a framework, for the document. I simply sat at the computer and started with the first page — the Table of Contents — and removed whatever was not pertinent to what I wanted to do. Within an hour, I had my own Table of Contents. From there, I simply created a title page for each line item.

Sample Table of Contents

If you have followed the steps outlined earlier in this section, you will already have most of the content to drop into your plan. After that comes some deeper digging. Talk to experts in your industry to fill in the holes. You will know the questions. Do your homework. Once you have crafted your plan, ask your accountability partners to review it before giving it to the bank! Step by step, word-by-word, it will all come together.

When I presented my business plan to the four lending institutions I had identified, I was asking for a million-dollar investment. I was scared to death. But I had done my homework, became an expert in my field, and could address all the questions they threw my way. Thankfully, I did the work to prepare myself to be taken seriously. My "pipe dream" was closer to reality and I had a good idea what I was talking about.

As I walked through the discussions with the banks, each commented on how well put together the business plan for Tiffany Hill was. I discovered from conversations with these bankers that business plans run the gamut from hand-written three-page documents to multi-level documents spanning hundreds of pages. The larger the investment you are seeking, the more polished your plan will need to be.

Here are a couple of suggestions for your plan development:

• Always appear professional in your request.
• Say what you need to say making sure you convey the situation and need — then stop.

- Sometimes less said is better. Know when to stop writing. Do not enter the state of perpetual planning.

Create a solid document that you feel good about and then start applying to lending institutions. You have done the work — don't be afraid! The worst they can say is "no." You will be no worse off than when you applied. In fact, you might gain insights based on the reasons for their rejection. If you should be rejected, improve your plan with the feedback you received and try again.

During their evaluation process, the banks will certainly query you for additional information. Allow your plan to grow based on their requests. In my case, the bank asked for two additional documents: a chronological listing of all my initiatives related to my pursuit of a B&B and a SWOT (strengths, weaknesses, opportunities, and threats) analysis. Here's what I added:

Background

Building the B&B on Tiffany Hill will fulfill a 25 year dream in the making. As the journey unfolded, there were many initiatives undertaken to prepare myself for the end result. This also includes extensive travel of bed and breakfasts both domestically and abroad over the years.

1985 — Focused travel to bed & breakfast commenced.

1994 — Attended Oates & Bedfedlt seminar on How to Purchase a B&B.

1995 — Built my home to expose myself to the building aspects.

1997 — Turned my hobby of stained glass into a sideline business.

1999 — Launched the Dreambuilders Fund taking deposits for rooms. Formed the Buck Wisers Investment Club to learn about the stock market. Attended National B&B Conference in Nashville, TN.

2000 — Pulled together Idea Book creating the vision of the facility & decor.

2001 — Established an automatic investment plan saving up to 37%.

2002 — Stayed the investment course & grew the stained glass business.

2003 — Started inn sitting for The Secret Garden B&B in Weaverville, NC

2004 — Attended the NC B&B Association Conference & continued inn sitting. Worked with graphic designer to develop business logos.

2005 — Extended inn sitting services to B&Bs in the Asheville market. Developed the floor plan for the B&B on Tiffany Lane. Developed initial business plan. Closed Dreambuilder fund with $10,000.

2006 — Moved to North Carolina. Started property search. Increased savings to 50%.

2007 — Attended the National PAII Conference in Myrtle Beach. Established Advisory Board. Located B& B mentor who has built a 7 room bed & breakfast in Virginia. Created LLC & set up accounting system.

A SWOT analysis is a structured planning method used to evaluate the strengths, weaknesses, opportunities, and threats to your business goal.

Sample SWOT Analysis

Strengths	Weaknesses
Location Established tourism Marketing acumen Airport Major interstates Pastoral setting Proximity to dining Multiplicity of attractions New construction	New B&B Lack of name recognition
Urban markets within 2-4 hour radius New corporations Experiential travel Local B&B network Colleges Summer camp parents	Uncontrolled start up expenses Competition Other lodging pricing
Opportunities	**Threats**

Although it appears daunting, it really is easy to create a business plan. Hopefully, this chapter has taken some of the mystery out of it for you. The unknown can be such a deterrent at times. All you need to do is start. One word at a time, one document at a time, and before you know it, your plan will materialize. Roll up your sleeves and get started.

It's Your Turn. What's The Worst That Can Happen?

Remember the answer to your question, "What is the worst thing that can happen if you try?" Hopefully that will propel you to success and to the fulfillment of why you are walking on this earth!

The world is full of ordinary people like me who, with the right focus, can do extraordinary things. Remember the crossroad I faced when I lost my job in 2007? I had a choice: look for another job or go in the direction of my dream. I took a step of faith toward my dream, got a million-dollar loan while I was unemployed, bought six acres of land somewhere I didn't know a soul, built the first B&B invited into the Southern Living Hotel Collection while I was collecting unemployment, and opened my doors to a full house. I took my dream, laid down my will, and picked up God's will for my life. With a lot of focus, determination, and a big God, I was blessed to succeed. It has been a wonderful journey of welcoming people from all walks of life and providing them with a place of rest and restoration as they travel.

Today, after years of putting one foot in front of the other — letting the lamp light my path — I've reached a point where I am having the time of my life. I know without a doubt that I have done what I was put on this earth to do. That gives me a peace that surpasses all understanding.

Part III
Tiffany Hill as an
Inspiration to Others

Little did I know as I embarked upon making my dream come true that others might also be inspired by my journey to Tiffany Hill. The more I lived my dream and shared it with guests day in and day out as an innkeeper/proprietor, the more I realized that this journey was not about the making of a bed and breakfast.

The true legacy of Tiffany Hill is the opportunity to inspire others to take a step of faith to pursue what has been tugging at their heartstrings. One of the most wonderful aspects of innkeeping is welcoming guests who depart as friends. Two of those guests/friends were inspired by the story of Tiffany Hill and took a step of faith. Each pursued something that had been on their heart or in their minds for quite some time. Each of them succeeded, and with their permission I am able to provide a glimpse of their accomplishments.

A Change in Life's Direction, Chuck Baker

Earlier in this book, you might remember the mention of a couple from Chattanooga who found my B&B. That one couple has blessed Tiffany Hill beyond belief over the years by introducing their friends and family to my Dream Come True! Little did we know that God's blessings would flow in both directions. As time unfolded and the connection between Tiffany Hill and the Bakers grew, life as they knew it would also drastically change.

From the moment Chuck Baker first set foot on Tiffany Hill, to him it seemed to be a place of solitude, a place of rest, a place of healing, and a place of dreams.

It was November 2009 when he and his wife, Cynthia, first became our guests. He says, in retrospect, that it was clear that the timing of their stay was providentially ordained. In God's perfect sovereignty, He intertwined their lives with mine for encouragement and support at a tender time in the life of Tiffany Hill. When we met, Chuck was an executive for the country's largest disability insurance carrier, a Fortune 250 company. That year, 2009, Chuck had experienced several unexpected hardships and stresses related to family, health, and career. He and Cynthia needed a retreat from their family and corporate pressures. They were desperately hoping that the Bed & Breakfast on Tiffany Hill could provide that place of physical and spiritual renewal.

Guests were few and far between in the early days, so on that first visit, the Bakers had the whole B&B to themselves. Over the course of their four-day stay, we had plenty of time to get to know one another and solidify the foundation of a friendship between us. It was during that stay that Chuck and Cynthia began to hear about my planning, preparation, and ultimate realization of my dream — the Bed & Breakfast on Tiffany Hill. They heard about my trust in God and my faith journey in building Tiffany Hill. As we talked, we both realized that we were like-minded in our Christian faith and Chuck began to share his dream — to one day leave the corporate world and use his God-given gifts for ministry.

I recall that as our relationship grew over time, at one point I shared with Chuck and Cynthia my perspective that when you join God on the path He has mapped out for you, you need to hold on! It will be like the vertebrae of your spine lining up perfectly and the Holy Spirit shooting straight through you, opening up paths and directions you never thought possible — making your way easy without burden.

The Bakers shared that one of the aspects of their life situation that would need to fall into place in order for them to take a giant step of faith toward ministry would be the sale of their home. Do you remember the housing market in 2010? One word . . . dismal! But not for God! One day, Chuck and Cynthia received a note in their mailbox from someone who was offering to purchase their home. They hadn't even put it on the market yet! Miraculously, the offer was for full value of what they would want and need to take a step of faith. Like I said, when you join God on the path He has for you, He will make the way straight and easy.

Their visits to Tiffany Hill did not disappoint in providing a place for rest, restoration, and yes, a place to dream. God used their time here to begin Chuck and Cynthia's preparation of a major life and career change just 12 months later. According to Chuck, "In a truly miraculous way, God opened the door for me to take early retirement and leave a successful business career to step out in faith and lead a non-denominational, Christian children's home in Chattanooga, Tennessee." He became President and CEO of Bethel Bible Village, a 60+ year-old ministry whose mission is to provide safe, nurturing, Christ-centered homes for children of families in crisis.

Over the years, Chuck and Cynthia have truly become part of the Tiffany Hill family. In the first five years, they were responsible for bringing more than 200 room nights to Tiffany Hill by inviting their friends and family. Without their support, I am truly not sure if my journey on Tiffany Hill would have lasted past the first six months. God knits us together for His good in more ways than one. It was during their initial visit in 2009 that the inspiration and confidence to dream the impossible became a reality as the Bakers began to step out in faith and trust God's plan for their lives.

"Tiffany Hill is more than a building. It is a home, inviting guests to enjoy the rolling green hills of North Carolina, the peace and tranquility of the front porch, the fabulous three-course breakfasts, and Selena's gracious hospitality," Chuck says. "But for me, to quote a phrase from an old hymn, Tiffany Hill is 'a place of quiet rest, near to the heart of God.'"

If reading Chuck's story moves you and you want to find out more about Bethel Bible Village, please feel free to contact them. They do an amazing job of providing homes to children whose families are in crisis.

Bethel Bible Village
3001 Hamill Rd.
Hixson, TN 37343
(423) 842-5757
www.bethelbiblevillage.org

Dream of Publishing a Book,
Susan Hallman Terrana

During her career in corporate America, Susan Hallman Terrana lived and worked in Manhattan. The street performers and people of New York fascinated her with all their unique personalities. It was during this period of her life that the first thoughts of publishing a book came to mind. She took the next step and discussed it with friends and relatives. While everyone thought it was a great idea, they, like Susan, had no real concept of how to go about making a book — much less about getting it published. The intriguing concept was overwhelming to pursue at the time and ended up resting on Susan's shelf of "sweet dreams."

Fast forward to August 2010, when Susan discovered the Bed & Breakfast on Tiffany Hill while perusing Facebook. Shortly thereafter, she gathered her friends and booked a Girl-friend's Pajama Party on Tiffany Hill. From the moment she walked through the front door of the B&B, it was love at first sight. She enjoyed what she describes as the beauty, Southern hospitality, and amazing breakfasts at Tiffany Hill. There was never a doubt in her mind she would return after that weekend. So in October 2011, she came back with her husband to celebrate their wedding anniversary.

Sitting at breakfast one morning, the table discussion centered on taking the recipes served during breakfast at Tiffany Hill and publishing a cookbook. The idea of all of the beautiful dishes springing to life on the pages of a cookbook with photos of the B&B and the gardens made Susan's heart soar. As the images danced in her mind, Susan's head turned so quickly to catch my attention that it caught me off guard. So I asked her if she might be interested in helping me pull together a cookbook for Tiffany Hill. At first, she was intrigued with the project and said yes. It sounded like such fun. But then it happened again — the fear of the unknown crept into her mind. Where to begin? There was a voice inside of Susan screaming, "Yes, yes, this is so exciting!" Then another voice countering with, "No, no ABSOLUTELY NOT!"

After considerable thought, prayer, and some encouragement from her family, she asked herself the pivotal question — "What is the worst thing that could happen?" Her biggest fear was in disappointing people. I told her that no one would even need to know we were working on this project at first. I suggested she simply take the initial step and start with some research on what it would take to publish a cookbook. Slowly but surely, she did take that first step and overcame the voices of doubt in her head. She researched different types of publishing and what was involved. After a couple of weeks of Internet searches, bookstore visits, and telephone inquiries to different publishers, she was convinced that this cookbook was an impossible task.

But timing is everything! If God wants something done, He will open the doors. Just when she was about to give up, someone stopped by the B&B wanting to discuss a travel book for North Carolina. After listening to his project, I asked if he might be willing to talk to Susan regarding our publishing project. He agreed and that one call between them changed the entire course of events. He spent time answering her questions and gave her the contact information for a good-fit publishing company. This man — who seemingly appeared from out of the blue — gave Susan exactly what she needed to take the next step for this project to become a reality: confidence!

"Some day I may do a book of my own," Susan says, "but if I don't, I will always have Breakfast at Tiffany Hill and the pride of our accomplishment."

A few lessons Susan learned from her journey turning a publishing dream into a reality:

- The hardest part of tackling the unknown is taking that first step.
- Trust that if you are heading down a path that is intended for you, God will show you the way.
- Have confidence in your abilities. You can do more than you ever thought possible.
- It's impossible to be successful without teamwork.
- Positive reinforcement and encouragement from others is very important along your journey.

- You are never too old to stretch yourself and learn new things.
- How do you eat an elephant? One bite at a time.
- It's better to try and fail than never to have tried.
- The feeling of pride and accomplishment when you do something that you thought was impossible is amazing!

Third Person/Special Request

When I started focusing on what *Courage is Abundant in the Abstract* would look like, I envisioned this last section with three stories of people who had been inspired by my journey to Tiffany Hill. Two of those stories have now been shared — one was a major change in life direction and the other an accomplishment of a project.

I was considering whose story would be my third when it dawned on me: That third person is you! Write your own story. Take what I have shared with you and bring to life what has been placed on your heart. Take that first step of faith. And when you do, please let me know. You will complete the circle.

I'm looking forward to hearing from you!

Selena Einwechter
c/o Bed & Breakfast on Tiffany Hill
400 Ray Hill Road
Mills River, NC 28759

In Closing

So there you have it — the story of my faith journey, along with some concrete ideas and steps to start you on your own path. Hopefully this book has accomplished what I set out to achieve: to inspire you to take the first steps toward your Dream Come True. Equally important was to give you some tools to get started. After all, what good is a dose of inspiration without knowing the next step? Now I hope you will put this book down and start! Grab a piece of paper or fire up your computer and write whatever you are inspired to write.

Maybe your first step is a Mind Dump of all the things swirling in your head that need to be done. Or, possibly you are ready to develop the initial timeline of your desired achievement or goal. Whatever it is, simply start.

Here's one last word to keep at the forefront of your mind to help you along the way: FOCUS. Life is full! Only you can keep yourself on the track toward your dream or goal. If your dream is important to you, you must stay focused. I guarantee you that the more you focus, the more things will start happening. One day you will look back, like I do, in total amazement! You, my friend, will be living your dream!

Focus is Key

So, whatever it is — just start. Today. Now. This minute! Get going. You can do it. Now, where is that piece of paper?

Dreams & Goals Realized

Once you arrive at your destination or desired result, know that it is not the end but a new beginning, which, by the way, continues to unfold with new challenges and opportunities every day. Just because you achieve what you dreamed of does not mean that the journey is over. You will reach a new plateau and chances are you will see a new goal in front of you. It is all good. Isn't life wonderful? It is so full of new beginnings every day. The good news is you will know how to get started because you have been at the beginning before. Congratulations! You are living your dream!

> *"You are never too old to set another goal or to dream a new dream!"* — *C.S. Lewis*

Sequel to
Breakfast at Tiffany Hill

Once Tiffany Hill was open for business, guests would frequently ask for our recipes. At first I would simply photocopy them and leave the recipe in their suites as a surprise. As guests continued to ask, they would also suggest that we do a cookbook. So, in 2012, we published Breakfast at Tiffany Hill; Experience the Dream.

By the time the cookbook was published, we started to tire of our original set of recipes — so we developed new ones. Of course the next question became, "Is this in the cookbook?" With that said, we offer what we call the Sequel to Breakfast at Tiffany Hill with this collection of post-cookbook recipes for our beloved guests to enjoy.

Table of Contents

Frosted Grapes

- 12 grapes/person being served
- ⅓ cup butter, softened
- ½ cup powdered sugar
- ½ cup sour cream
- ¼ teaspoon vanilla

Beat together butter and powdered sugar until smooth. Add sour cream and vanilla and beat until creamy. Cover and chill until ready to serve. Then mix a small amount with grapes (about 1 tablespoon) until grapes are coated. Refrigerate remaining frosting for future use. Serve in sugar-rimmed martini glasses and adorn with mint leaf!

*"We must begin where we are and
step in the direction of our lives."*

Minted Grapefruit

- ½ cup grapefruit/person being served
- 2 tablespoons honey
- 2 tablespoons fresh mint, chopped

Combine honey and chopped mint with juice from grapefruit. Stir until well mixed, then pour back over grapefruit sections. Chill and serve for a delightful summer fruit!

"Don't settle for where you are if that is not where you want to be."

Pineapple with Honey Rum Sauce

- fresh pineapple, cut in chunks
- 1 stick butter
- ½ cup brown sugar
- ¼ cup dark rum

Melt butter and brown sugar in a saucepan. Stir in rum until well combined. Spoon warm sauce over fresh pineapple chunks. Serves 12

"Life is a blank palette.
It is what you choose to make of it that counts."

Warm Berries and Yogurt

- ⅓ cup frozen mixed berries/person
- Vanilla yogurt

In a saucepan, add 1/3 cup per person of frozen berries. Cook on medium heat until berries start to render juice. Stir lightly, being careful not to mash berries. Once heated thoroughly, serve over vanilla yogurt. Serves 1

"Fear and doubt often cause us to dismiss our ideas or downsize them to fit our consciousness."

Blueberry Banana French Toast

- 3 sliced bananas
- 1 loaf French bread, cubed
- 6 eggs
- 3 cups milk
- ½ cup sugar
- 2 teaspoon cinnamon
- 1 teaspoon vanilla
- ¼ teaspoon nutmeg
- salt — a pinch
- 1 cup blueberries
- 1 tablespoon sugar
- 1 teaspoon cinnamon
- maple syrup, for drizzling

Spray a 9 x 13 glass dish with cooking spray. Layer the bananas into the bottom of the dish. Top with the cubed bread. Combine the eggs, milk, sugar, cinnamon, vanilla, nutmeg and salt, then pour over the bread and press down to coat. Spread the blueberries on top of the mixture. Combine the sugar and cinnamon and sprinkle over the blueberries. Bake at 350 for 45 minutes, or until berries are bursting. Serve with maple syrup. Serves 8-10

"Open yourself to God's lead."

Cinnamon Swirl Stuffed French Toast with Warm Berry Compote Syrup*

- 12 slices cinnamon raisin bread
- 8 oz cream cheese
- 3 tablespoon sugar
- 4 eggs
- ¼ cup milk; ¼ cup half and half
- 1 teaspoon vanilla

Blend cream cheese and sugar. Spread onto bread. Place 6 slices of bread, cream cheese side up, into 8 inch square pan, sprayed with cooking spray. Cover with remaining bread slices, cream cheese side down. Whisk eggs, milk, half and half and vanilla until well-blended; pour over bread. Cover and refrigerate overnight.

In the morning, heat oven to 350 and bake french toast uncovered 30-35 minutes. Cut diagonally; serve dusted with powdered sugar and berry compote on side.

*Berry Compote Syrup

- ½ cup berry compote (equal parts jelly & water)
- ½ cup maple syrup

Mix together and heat on stovetop. Add fresh berries if desired. Serves 6

"Waiting is an action verb! It is a choice.

Cranberry Orange French Toast

- 1 loaf French bread, cubed
- 6 eggs
- 4 cup half and half
- 1 cup dried cranberries
- 1 10-oz jar orange marmalade
- ½ cup pure maple syrup

Arrange half of the French bread in a lightly greased 13 x 9 pan. Sprinkle with half of the cranberries and top with remaining bread and cranberries. Whisk together eggs and half and half and pour over the bread mixture, pressing down to soak. Let rest at least 30 minutes. Bake covered at 350 for 25 minutes. Uncover and bake 20 more minutes. Heat syrup and marmalade on stovetop and serve over toast. Serves 10

"Knowledge will help fuel your confidence
and propel you to take another step."

Crème Brulee French Toast

- 1 ¾ sticks butter
- 2 cups packed brown sugar
- 2 loaves uncut French Bread (12 slices)
- 10 eggs
- 2 cups half and half
- 1 cup milk
- 1 tablespoon Grand Marnier
- 2 teaspoon vanilla
- ½ teaspoon salt
- 1 tablespoon corn syrup

Melt butter with brown sugar and corn syrup, stirring until smooth. Pour into 13 x 9 glass dish, sprayed with cooking spray. Cut 1 inch slices of bread and arrange in one layer in dish. In a bowl, whisk together eggs, milk, half and half, vanilla, Grand Marnier and salt until combined. Pour over the bread and chill overnight. Bake in 350 oven about 30 minutes until puffed and slightly golden. Serves 12

"If something is important to you,
you will need to focus on it for it to come to pass."

Mixed Berry Stuffed Crepes *(two crepes per person)*

Filling
- 4 oz cream cheese
- 2 tablespoon confectioners sugar
- 1 tablespoon lemon juice

Berry Sauce

- 3 cups mixed berries (blueberries, strawberries, blackberries)
- ½ cup sugar, ½ cup water
- ¼ teaspoon ground cinnamon

Prepare ready made crepes by wrapping in foil and putting in warming drawer or oven. Mix berry sauce on stovetop until bubbly; set aside. Prepare filling, mixing until fluffy; spread thinly on crepes.

To serve, fold crepes in quarters and lay them atop each other. Pour warm berry sauce on top and garnish with fresh berries. Serves 6.

"God will give you more than you think you can handle because He wants you to mature."

Baked Scrambled Eggs

- 8 oz cream cheese
- ½ cup half and half
- 3 tablespoon butter, melted
- 12 eggs

Preheat oven to 350. Pour the melted butter into a 9 x 13 glass casserole dish.

Place cream cheese in a microwave-safe mixing bowl and heat for 2 minutes, covered, at 50% heat. Stir the cream cheese with a whisk. Microwave an additional minute at 50% heat, or until thoroughly creamy. Add half and half to cream cheese and mix until well combined. Pour mixture into the pan with butter.

Using the same mixing bowl, beat the eggs and pour into the casserole dish, blending together. Bake for 10 minutes, then stir. Continue cooking for 15 more minutes, stirring every 5 minutes. Serves 8-10

"Begin with the end in sight."

Baked Potato Egg Cups

- 2 frozen potato cups/person
- Salt & Pepper
- Spray Olive Oil
- White queso
- Shredded ham
- Fresh chives
- TH's Baked Scrambled Eggs (see recipe)

Prepare TH's Baked Scrambled Eggs. While baking, prepare Potato Cups by spraying the inside of the cups with Olive Oil spray. Put face down onto pan. Pour olive oil into hand and spread over the outside of the potato cups. Sprinkle with salt and pepper lightly. Bake at 375 for 45 minutes or until edges are turning brown.

While eggs and potato cups bake, take shredded ham and put into a dish with a small amount of water. Cover with lid and put in microwave for 1 minute to steam. Then place ham inside the baked potato cups and top with eggs. Heat the queso in microwave, then spoon over the eggs, letting the queso soak down into the potato cups. Sprinkle tops with fresh chives. Serves 1

"We are all purposed for this life."

Biscuits and Gravy

- 12 frozen biscuits
- gravy packet
- sausage, precooked and frozen, chopped

Take biscuits out of freezer the night prior to cooking. In the morning, cook gravy according to package directions. (For 6-8, the smaller portion measurements are fine). Set aside, off the heat.

Sprinkle a little flour on a cutting board and lightly coat each biscuit on both sides so that you can stretch the dough. (DO NOT OVERWORK THE DOUGH) Form the biscuits into muffin tins sprayed with Pam. Let the sides of the biscuit rest on the top of the pan. Sprinkle enough sausage into the bottom of each cup to cover the dough. Ladle about 2 scoops of gravy into each muffin cup, being cautious not to overfill the cups.

Bake at 350 degrees for 20-25 minutes, until crust is golden brown. When removed from oven and placed on plate (2/ guest), ladle gravy into the tops of each muffin cup, not letting it pour over the edges. Serve with scrambled eggs and sliced tomatoes for a savory delight! Serves 6

"Finding what God designed you to do on this earth will be the most important and freeing event of your life."

Broccoli Cheddar Quiche

- 1 prepared pie crust
- ½ cup cubed white cheddar cheese
- ½ cup shredded cheddar cheese
- ½ cup roughly chopped broccoli, cooked slightly
- 8 eggs
- 1 cup half & half
- ½ cup milk
- ¼ teaspoon nutmeg
- ½ teaspoon season salt
- 2 dashes Texas Pete

Preheat oven to 375. Fit pie crust into pie plate. Evenly spread both cheeses and the broccoli onto the pie crust. Mix next ingredients together and pour the mixture over the cheese and broccoli. Bake for 45 minutes or until golden brown and set in the middle. Serves 6-8

"Each of our paths unfold at the time appointed."

Caprese Strata

- 4 mini ciabatta loafs, cut into small cubes
- 2 tablespoon prepared pesto
- ½ cup mozzarella cheese
- ¼ cup parmesan cheese
- 6 eggs
- ¾ cup half and half
- ½ cup milk
- 2 large tomatoes, sliced

Place half of the cubed bread in a pie pan that has been sprayed with cooking oil. Sprinkle with ¼ cup mozzarella cheese. Arrange remaining bread on top. Whisk together eggs, half & half, milk, and pesto. Pour over bread, pressing down to absorb egg mixture. Arrange tomato slices evenly over the top of the bread. Sprinkle with remaining mozzarella and parmesan. Cover and chill overnight. In the morning, bake at 350 for 45 minutes. Serves 6-8

*"God's plans for you are far bigger
and greater than you could ever imagine."*

Egg Puffs

- 1 full sheet of puff pastry
- 1 cup shredded cheddar cheese
- ¼ cup crumbled bacon
- 12 oz cream cheese
- ¼ cup milk

- 4 eggs
- 4 tablespoon green peppers, finely chopped
- 2 tablespoon red peppers, finely chopped

Cut the full sheet of pastry in half and continue quartering until the sheet is 16 individual rectangles. Stretch dough in 2 directions and press into greased muffin tins, allowing edges to hang over. Sprinkle an even amount of cheese and bacon into each cup. Put the cream cheese into a microwave safe bowl, covered, for 2 minutes on 50% power. Whisk until smooth, then add the milk and whisk again. Add the eggs and beat until smooth, then add the peppers. Ladle egg mixture evenly into the cups. (It is fine if the mixture runs into the pan!) Pull the edges of the pastry up and pinch the four corners together. Bake uncovered at 375 for 18-22 minutes or until golden brown. Serves 8 (2 puffs/person)

"God orchestrates our experiences to equip us for the future."

Greek Potato Tart

- ½ onion, finely chopped
- ¼ cup red peppers, finely chopped
- 1 cup mushrooms, finely chopped
- 1 tablespoon olive oil
- 1 cup spinach, chopped
- 8 eggs
- ¼ cup water
- Dash of nutmeg
- 4 oz tomato basil feta

Potato crust

- ¼ cup shredded hashbrowns
- ¾ cup parmesan cheese
- 2 tablespoon flour
- 2 tablespoon +/- water

Sauté onion, red peppers and mushrooms in olive oil. In separate pan, sauté spinach, then add to the onion mixture. Set aside. Combine all crust ingredients and mix by hand. Pat evenly into large greased muffin tins to create a crust. Mix the eggs, water and nutmeg together. Add the feta cheese, then the onion/mushroom mixture. Stir together then ladle over the potato crust. Bake at 375 for 20 minutes. Serves 12

"God supplies you when He calls you."

Savory Bread Pudding

- 1 tablespoon olive oil
- 4 oz sliced portabella mushrooms
- ½ tablespoon minced garlic
- 1 cup milk
- 1 cup heavy whipping cream
- Salt & Pepper
- 1/8 teaspoon ground nutmeg
- 4 eggs
- 4 large croissants, cut into ½" pieces
- ¼ cup butter, melted
- 1 ½ cups swiss cheese
- ½ lb asparagus (approx. 12 stalks), peeled and sliced into 1" pieces
- 1 ½ cups diced ham

Mince mushrooms & sauté with olive oil until water is rendered and they start to brown. Add garlic & cook another 30 seconds. Remove from heat. Saute the asparagus pieces in a very small amount of olive oil until crisp tender; then set aside. Combine milk, cream, salt, pepper & nutmeg, then heat until mixture is barely simmering. Toss the croissant pieces with melted butter. Fold mushroom mixture, asparagus & cheese together. Slowly add eggs to the milk mixture then pour over croissants. Spoon into greased ramekins. Bake at 325 for 30 minutes. Serves 8

"Start today! This very minute! For what you envision —
for your future."

Tomato Onion Tart

- ½ sheet puff pastry
- 1 sweet onion
- 4 tomatos
- ½ cup mozzarella cheese
- ½ cup parmesan cheese
- 2 tablespoon fresh oregano

Stretch pastry into pie plate, leaving edges hanging over. Cut tomatoes and let drain on paper towels while cutting onion into slices. Sprinkle half of the mozzarella cheese into bottom of pastry, then half of the parmesan. Top with tomatoes and onions, then repeat layers. Sprinkle top with oregano and pull up edges of pastry lightly to cover the pie.

Bake at 350 for 30 minutes or until golden brown. Serves 6-8

"New beginnings come from some other beginning's end."

Zucchini-Onion Frittata

- 3 tablespoon butter
- 2 tablespoon vegetable oil
- 2 medium zucchini, thinly sliced
- 1 medium onion, cut in half and thinly sliced
- ½ cup grated Parmesan cheese, divided
- 8 eggs
- ¼ cup milk
- 2 teaspoons of seasoned salt
- ¼ cup chopped fresh basil
- Plum or grape tomatoes for garnish

Melt butter with oil in a 12" iron frying pan. Add zucchini & onion; saute 12-14 minutes or until onion is tender. Remove from heat; stir in ¼ cup Parmesan cheese. Whisk eggs, milk and seasoned salt and pour over vegetable mixture. Bake at 350 for 13-15 minutes or until set; Sprinkle evenly with remaining ¼ cup Parmesan cheese and basil. Garnish with tomatoes.

Serve with smoked sausage and sliced tomatoes. Serves 8

"The secret in succeeding is in trying.
Failure is in not trying."

Berry Cream Delight

- 1 box instant vanilla pudding
- 1 cup cold milk
- 1 cup sour cream
- 1 cup blueberries
- ¼ cup graham cracker crumbs

Stir together pudding mix and milk. Fold in sour cream. Chill.

Using petit wine glasses, put 2 blueberries into the bottom and top with a spoonful of the chilled mixture. Alternate blueberries and cream mixture until glass is full. Sprinkle lightly with graham cracker crumbs and enjoy! Serves 12-14

"Surrendering to God's plan is not just a one-time choice. Rather, it is a life-long process."

Derby Pie

- ½ pound butter, melted in microwave
- 1 cup sugar
- ½ cup flour
- 2 eggs, beaten
- 1 teaspoon vanilla
- 1 cup walnuts or pecans, chopped fine
- 1 cup chocolate chips
- 1 unbaked pie shell

Mix all ingredients in the order listed and pour into unbaked pie shell. Bake at 375 for 30-35 minutes. Serve warm. Serves 8.

"Focus is key. All you need to do is start.
Roll up your sleeves and get started."

Frozen Peach Pie

- 1 10-ounce can frozen peach daiquiri mix
- 1 14-ounce can sweetened condensed milk
- 1 8-ounce container of Cool Whip
- 1 Graham Cracker Pie Crust

Mix first two ingredients until combined. Fold in Cool Whip. Put filling into pie crust. Freeze overnight.

Take out 5 minutes before ready to serve to cut. Serve with whipped cream on top. Serves 12

*"Listen for discernment of knowing
you are going in the right direction."*

Grandma's Peach Cobbler

- 1 can peaches (or can use 2 cups fresh fruit)
- ½ cup sugar
- 1 stick butter

Batter

- ½ cup sugar
- ½ cup flour
- 1 teaspoon baking powder
- ½ cup milk

Melt butter in a 9x9 Pyrex dish in microwave. Mix peaches and ½ cup sugar together and pour over butter. Mix batter ingredients and pour over peaches in a drizzle fashion. Bake at 375 for 30 minutes. Allow to rest 15 minutes before serving, as fruit will be piping hot!

Serve with dab of ice cream on top. Serves 10-12.

"Focus is Key"

Lemon Coconut Trifle

- 2 (10-ounce) jars lemon curd
- 1 container Cool Whip, thawed
- 1 (8-ounce) loaf angel food cake, cut into ½ inch cubes
- 1 cup toasted sweetened flake coconut

In a medium bowl, stir together lemon curd and ½ cup Cool Whip.

Using small dessert dishes, layer angel food cake, lemon curd mixture, remaining Cool Whip and coconut as desired. Serves 12

"Faith is stepping on a path that is unseen."

Lime Pot de Crème

- 2 cups heavy whipping cream
- 1 cup caster sugar or super fine sugar
- 1/3 cup lime juice
- Blueberries or Mint to garnish

In a large bowl, combine the cream and sugar and stir until sugar dissolves. Blend in lime juice. Pour into shallow ramekins and freeze until firm. Garnish and enjoy! Serves 8

"To succeed, you must begin or you will remain frozen in your current dimension."

Little Pineapple Upside Down Cakes

- 1 tablespoon butter
- 1 tablespoon light corn syrup
- 2 tablespoon light brown sugar
- 1 pineapple slice, well drained
- ½ maraschino cherries, well drained
- 1 Frozen Biscuit

Spray 1 individual sized trifle dish with cooking spray. In small bowl, microwave the butter, corn syrup and brown sugar until bubbly. Pour into trifle dish. Top with pineapple slice and insert cherry into center of ring. Top with frozen biscuit. Bake at 375 for 20-25 minutes or until deep golden brown. Let cool 5 minutes, then flip onto plate. Serves 1

"As you step toward your dream, take action on the things that you are able to do and let God take care of the rest."

Pecan Pie

- 3 eggs, well beaten
- 1 Cup white Karo syrup
- 3 tablespoon butter, melted
- 1 teaspoon vanilla
- ½ cup sugar
- ¼ teaspoon salt
- 1 cup pecans, chopped
- 1 pie crust

Combine all ingredients, beating well as each is added. Place in unbaked pie shell. Bake at 350 degrees for 45-55 minutes. Pecan filling should not jiggle or it needs to bake just a bit longer. Serves 12

"Life is about choices — what we choose to think and what we say. We become what we say and do."

Triple Chocolate Decadence

- 1 box brownie mix — prepared as directed and cut into circles using a biscuit cutter or rim of drinking glass
- 4 ounces white chocolate, finely chopped
- 8 oz cream cheese

Godiva Sauce

- ¼ cup whipping cream
- ¼ cup dark chocolate, melted
- 1 tablespoon Godiva

Mix together white chocolate and cream cheese and set aside. Mix Godiva sauce over heat until bubbling. Set aside. Spread one brownie circle with white chocolate mixture and layer 2nd brownie circle on top. Put on plate and top with hot Godiva sauce. Sprinkle with diced strawberries to garnish. Serves 12-18

"Time once spent can never be regained — use your time wisely."

Tropical Fruit Pie

- 1 14-ounce can sweetened condensed milk
- 1 12-ounce Cool Whip, thawed
- 1 20-ounce can crushed pineapple, drained
- 2 tablespoons lemon juice
- ½ cup mashed ripe banana
- 1 can mandarin oranges, drained
- ½ cup chopped walnuts
- ½ cup maraschino cherries
- 2 graham cracker pie crusts

In a large bowl, stir together condensed milk and Cool Whip. Fold in next six ingredients. Pour evenly into graham cracker crusts. Cover and freeze overnight or until firm. Remove from freezer 10 minutes before serving. Serves 12

"Dreams give us hope for a better tomorrow."

About the Author

After spending more than thirty years in corporate America, Selena Einwechter decided to take a leap of faith and pursue her dream: building her own bed & breakfast. In June of 2009, Selena opened the doors of Tiffany Hill, a B&B in the foothills of the Blue Ridge Mountains near Asheville, NC. Selena loves to tell the story of how her dream became a reality. In fact, she finds that she is spending a great deal of time sharing the process she created with others.

Today, the Bed and Breakfast on Tiffany Hill is a thriving inn with seven grand suites and a roster of media accolades that stretches from Every Day With Rachael Ray to Southern Living and the Wall Street Journal. Selena is in her element as she welcomes guests, cooks delicious breakfasts, and plumps pillow for the sweet dreams of weary travelers.

> *"I have peace in knowing that I fulfilled*
> *what I was placed on this earth to do."*
>
> —*Selena Einwechter*